Elementary School Secretaries

Elementary School Secretaries

The Women in the Principal's Office

Ursula Casanova

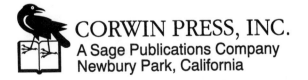

CORWIN PRESS, INC.
A Sage Publications Company
Newbury Park, California

For information address:

Corwin Press, Inc.
A Sage Publications Company
2455 Teller Road
Newbury Park, California 91320

SAGE Publications Ltd.
6 Bonhill Street
London EC2A 4PU
United Kingdom

SAGE Publications India Pvt. Ltd.
M-32 Market
Great Kailash I
New Delhi 110 048 India

Printed in the United States of America

Library of Congress Cataloging-in-Publication Data

Casanova, Ursula.
    Elementary school secretaries : the women in the principal's
office / Ursula Casanova.
       p. cm.
    Based on author's thesis (Ph. D.)—Arizona State University, 1985.
    Includes bibliographical references (p.) and index.
    ISBN 0-8039-3803-9. — ISBN 0-8039-3804-7 (pbk.)
    1. School secretaries—United States. 2. Elementary schools—
United States. I. Title.
LB2844.4.C37 1991
372.12'023—dc20
                                                  91-13613
                                                   CIP

FIRST PRINTING, 1991

Corwin Press Production Editor: Diane S. Foster

Contents

Preface

The five-year-old boy approached the counter with visible trepida-
tion: "Are you the office?" he asked the woman standing behind
the counter. Smiling broadly, she answered that she was. She
accepted the attendance register from him and thanked him profusely.

A girl walked into the office and asked to take the "principal's
challenge." The woman behind the desk greeted the girl by her first
name. Smiling, she walked around the desk to meet the girl by the
large wall map. The woman pointed to each of the states on the
United States map as the student identified them one by one. When
the girl had successfully named them all, the woman congratulated
her, gave her a hug and sent her off with a smile. Then she added
the child's name to the long list of successful challengers tacked
next to the wall map.

Unbeknownst to the five-year-old boy, his question crystallized
many popular perceptions of school secretaries. When visitors to a
school encounter that ubiquitous sign "Please report to the office,"
they report to the school secretary. When parents call the school
office, and when teachers and students speak of going to the office,
they are all referring to the school secretary. These women are the
protagonists in this book: *The women in the principal's office.*

WHY STUDY ELEMENTARY SCHOOL SECRETARIES?

My interest in elementary school secretaries is directly related to
my experience as an elementary school principal. I took over the
administration of an elementary school after the previous

principal's resignation. With only a year's experience as a vice-principal, it was a chaotic situation. The in-basket was full to overflowing. Much of what it contained bore little resemblance to the in-basket materials used in my university courses. But I was fortunate. The secretary was experienced and eager to be of assistance. She helped me to establish priorities, to understand the school's history, and to connect with the school and district staff. Through her and the equally competent secretaries who succeeded her in the job, I learned to trust, respect and rely on the person holding that position.

Several years later, I was involved in planning and monitoring research on school organization and administration. The attention of the educational research community was beginning to focus on the principal. I found the school secretary to be all but absent from that research. The principal, it appeared, was alone in the school office.

Years later, when it was my time to choose a research topic for my own graduate work, I considered the possibility of focusing on elementary school secretaries. I explored the idea by means of a series of observations and informal interviews with secretaries and principals in school offices. What I found out through these activities confirmed my decision to select elementary school secretaries as the topic for my doctoral dissertation. This book is a direct result of that work.

The absence of school secretaries from the scholarly literature says much about the prestige associated with that position. Researchers, it seems, have not attached much importance to their work. Principals are important, secretaries are not. As a researcher, I also suffered from these perceptions. For example, I submitted a paper on school secretaries to a national conference. It was rejected by one of the readers who deemed the topic to be irrelevant.

School secretaries are examples of the "thereness of women." They are compared by Lofland (1975) to the servants in mystery stories: They are always present but remain primarily part of the scene. They are ". . .essential to the set but largely irrelevant to the action. They are simply there" (p. 145).

In this regard school secretaries resemble not only other secretaries, but also the many women who work in the "helping professions": social workers, nurses, child- and geriatric-care workers, and many others. All of them occupy positions of responsibility that are undervalued by the society, though they are essential to its well being. Their status is low and their salaries lower; thus, in spite of their centrality they remain obscured, attracting little attention from researchers.

This book attempts to correct the record, first by acknowledging the presence of the elementary school secretary, and then by documenting the part she[1] plays in the school administration.

Multiple sets of data were used to compare the role of the secretary as performed and as perceived by different sources. My findings indicate a large discrepancy exists between the secretary's role as described in official sources such as job descriptions and textbooks, and the role as perceived by the secretaries themselves, their principals, and through my own observations. While official sources tend to ignore or trivialize the school secretary's role, secretaries, principals, and my own observations indicate that the secretary plays a critical role in a school's operation. Thus this book is meant to alert educators of all persuasions to the importance of the secretary's role in relation to the practical problems of school administration, and to the theoretical issues of research in schools.

Because elementary school secretaries are overwhelmingly female, this is also a book about women in the workplace. In this respect, I point out that these women, as well as many others in similar work situations, are placed in positions of "intermittent power." That is, they are expected to be compliant subordinates most of the time while simultaneously being able to take charge in the absence of the boss. This position requires exquisite balancing skills that are particularly compatible with the traditional roles assigned to women.

The elementary school as a workplace also places special demands on the women who work in school offices. Unlike their counterparts in business, these women must answer to a multi-layered clientele in an environment devoted to the nurturance of children. They are expected to assume any unassigned responsibilities and take care of whatever emergencies occur during the school day because they are "always there."

For this reason, I conclude that elementary school secretaries are more than office wives. They are more aptly described as "school mothers." It is a role that may have low status in society, but which appears to be essential in the culture of the school.

This book provides persuasive evidence for all these arguments. Much of the evidence comes through vignettes that capture moments in the daily life of elementary schools. Another portion comes through the voices of the principals and secretaries interviewed. And the results of a national survey supplement the qualitative data, allowing a broader view of the profession.

The book consists of five chapters in addition to the Preface, and the Appendix. Chapter 1 begins with a historical overview of the school secretary then traces the evolution of that role from its origins in the early 1920s to its present form. It is an interesting history with unexpected twists.

In Chapter 2, a framework helps the reader understand elementary school secretaries through their characteristics as females employed as clerical workers in elementary schools. This chapter also includes discussion of the group's demographics, and the characteristics of the group members' jobs, which is largely based on the secretaries' responses to a national survey. It also provides brief descriptions of the school settings where I conducted six case studies.

In Chapter 3, the reader will enter the school secretaries' world for a closer look at elementary school secretaries in their offices. That chapter will draw on data from my own observations and from interviews with secretaries and principals.

Chapter 4 focuses on the all-important relationship between the secretary and the principal. It also notes the surprisingly strong influence of the principal's gender on this relationship.

Chapter 5, the final chapter, summarizes the data, draws conclusions from my analysis and offers recommendations for practitioners and researchers.

NOTE

1. Although not all elementary school secretaries are female, the vast majority of them (99%) are. All the participants in this study were female. Therefore, female pronouns will be used throughout this book, both for reasons of style and to reflect reality.

Acknowledgments

The research reported in this book was born as a doctoral dissertation, but it did not begin there. As a school principal assisted by fine secretaries, I gained the experience that led me to the topic. Two of them, Lillian Silverstein and Josephine Manuse, helped me to see the world from the perspective of the elementary school secretary. Their help enabled me to define the questions that guided the study, and I thank them.

I was also fortunate to have the assistance of the National Association of Educational Office Personnel (NAEOP) and particularly of former presidents Patricia Fleming and Jeanne Haas. Fran Johnson, editor of the NAEOP's *The National Educational Office Secretary*, made available to me rare copies of the organization's early journals, which allowed me to trace the history of the profession. The assistance of all three in the preparation and completion of the survey was invaluable. I thank them.

Many other elementary school secretaries also contributed to this work. A large group of these very busy women was willing to give the time to answer the survey. Another six gave even more; they allowed me to share their workplace for many hours and submitted to lengthy interviews. For their hospitality and that of their principals who also welcomed me and answered my questions, I am deeply grateful.

I must also thank Susanne Shafer, Elizabeth Brandt, and Thomas Metos, all members of my doctoral committee as well as personal friends who influenced and guided the research reported here. From the beginning, they supported my ideas and encouraged me to pursue the topic. Nick Appleton, friend and boss, provided continuous support and encouragement, and patiently acceded to my demands for more powerful technology to assist me in the process.

I am also indebted to Dee Ann Spencer, friend and colleague, who gave of her time and experience to help me make this a better book. And no one could ask for a better research assistant than Sheila Chavez who never flagged in her pursuit of fugitive citations.

I am also appreciative for the assistance of my editor, C. Deborah Laughton, who believed in the worth of this work and encouraged me throughout its development.

Finally, throughout this effort I have been able to count on the love and support of my husband David, and our children Bethann, Lisa, Brett, Carlos and Leticia, the best "groupies" any author could have. They have reassured me when I flagged, and cheered when I succeeded. I thank them for their trust and patience.

About the Author

Ursula Casanova, Ph.D., has taught at all grade levels from primary school to university and adult education. She was an elementary school principal for five years. After a year as an Educational Policy Fellow at the National Institute of Education in Washington, DC, she became a Senior Research Associate at the same institute where she pursued research on the principalship. In 1985 Casanova completed her Ph.D. in Educational Foundations at Arizona State University. Between 1985 and 1987 she was both an Adjunct Professor in the College of Education and a Research Associate at the Bureau of Applied Research in Anthropology at the University of Arizona. At the end of that period she was awarded a post-doctoral fellowship at the Stanford University Center for Chicano Research. She is currently an Assistant Professor in the Department of Educational Leadership and Policy Studies at the College of Education of Arizona State University. Her research interests include school administration and organization, and issues of education and culture. With Virginia Richardson, Peggy Placier, and Karen Guilfoyle, she coauthored *Schoolchildren at Risk* (1989). Another book, *Putting Research to Work,* coauthored with David Berliner, is now in press.

For David and our children

A Historical Perspective of the School Secretary

What They Say about the School Secretary

The absence of the school secretary from research on school organization and administration, and particularly from research on elementary school principals, is puzzling. When principals are asked about the school secretary they will often say, "We couldn't run the school without her" or "She's the real boss here." A 1921 survey of elementary school principals suggests that these statements are more than empty rhetoric. Respondents to that survey indicated they would rather hire a new teacher than a new secretary (Church, 1971).

One of the few researchers who even mentions the school secretary is Wolcott (1973). In his extensive, descriptive study of an elementary school principal, he noted that the extent of the secretary's authority is a function of the location and activity of the principal. If the principal is present in the building, the secretary is restricted to monitoring messages and visits. But in the principal's absence, "even a decision on whether or not to make a decision could be important" (p. 131).

Wolcott might have been underestimating the role of the school secretary. The school office is the school's public face. Typically the only person there is the school secretary. All visitors, from elected representatives to delivery people, are requested to report to the office first. Their initial (sometimes only) contact with the school is through the school secretary. She is also in charge of distributing the mail and answering the telephone, so most of the information entering the school reaches her first. In addition, in schools where there are no vice-principals (68% of all elementary schools, according to the National Association of Elementary School Principals [Doud, 1988]), the secretary is likely to be the only adult in the office when the principal is out of the building. During those times, as noted by Wolcott (1973), she may be forced to make decisions the principal would normally be expected to make. Those decisions may have a large impact on the school and even on the school district.

The principals' tendency to value the assistance of their school secretaries is not reflected in the professional literature's many studies of elementary school principals. What were the origins of this role? When were secretaries first assigned to school offices? Why? How has this role evolved through the years?

How Elementary School Secretaries Came to Be: A Historical View

The melding of the school office and the person who performs its tasks is so complete that it is difficult to imagine a school without a secretary. And yet secretaries and school offices are comparatively recent additions to elementary schools. How, why, and when did school secretaries enter the educational scene?

The evolution of the elementary school secretary's position is intimately connected to that of the school principal. A glance at the development of the school principal's position is necessary in order to answer questions about the origins of the school secretary. This development can best be understood as an evolutionary process beginning with the simple organization of the one-room school and progressing to the administrative complexity of large urban schools. It is a process that also changed these educators from generalists to specialists.

Relieving principals for supervision

Educational tradition in the United States tends to look back fondly on the one-room schoolhouse. In those schools one teacher performed all duties necessary for the instructional welfare of one multiage group of students. There was no hierarchy and few administrative requirements. But by the turn of the century the school population was growing fast, particularly in urban areas. One-room schoolhouses were being replaced by multiclassroom schools, and urban schools especially became very large. Educators began to modify the simple organizational structure of the traditional school (Crouch, 1926).

As a result of these administrative pressures, the head or principal teacher emerged sometime around the middle of the nineteenth century. These teachers were assigned administrative responsibilities such as the maintenance of the school plant, attendance records and discipline. They were also expected to provide general instructional supervision for teaching assistants who also emerged around this time. These responsibilities entailed a higher salary and some professional recognition, but were to be fulfilled in addition to the teacher's duties in the classroom (Crouch, 1926).

From all-purpose teacher to teacher-principal

The lengthening list of duties assigned to the teacher-principal, coupled with administrative pressures due to increased enrollment and administrative demands, led educators to request at least partial relief from teaching responsibilities for principals. The need for instructional supervision was the main argument offered for this request.

The need for leadership was especially great in the larger urban schools. It was in those schools that relief was first provided. An 1871 board regulation for the city of St. Louis charged the principals with full responsibility for the internal government of their schools, provided there was no conflict with general regulations. It also included the proviso that the principals would be judged by the results produced by their schools' improvement. By 1933 to 1934 while more than 57% of the elementary school principals responding to a survey were teaching-principals; 70% of the principals in cities with populations larger than 100,000 had no teaching responsibilities (Goodykoontz & Lane, 1938).

The duties of building principals during this period were all-encompassing. They included handling all administrative details related to the work of janitors; responding to the needs of teachers;

overseeing the attendance, discipline and health of students; preparing, receiving and distributing orders and supplies; keeping inventories; maintaining the stock; maintaining records; and answering correspondence (Cubberley, 1923).

The similarity between many of these tasks and those later to be performed by elementary school secretaries is readily apparent. It also suggests the next logical step in this evolutionary process: the need to relieve the principal from "endless office routine and petty details" (Crouch, 1926, p. 213) that could be done by a clerk, thereby leaving the principal free to provide educational leadership (McClure, 1921; Gist, 1924; & McGill, 1926). In 1938, John A. Sexson, Superintendent of Pasadena, California schools, and then president of the American Association of School Administrators, stated that as educational programs had been "modernized," the principal had been taken out of the office and the school secretary had to assume many of his duties. These women, he added, were hired "in many cases with college and training equal to or superior to that possessed by teachers" (Sexson, 1938).

From teacher-principal to educational leader

The need for clerical help[1] in the elementary schools was the next focus for educators in search of the elusive goal of educational improvement. In fact the need for clerical assistance in the elementary schools was one of the main points of agreement among the founders of the National Education Association Department of Elementary School Principals (DESP).

Once again the larger schools in the country led in the provision of this assistance to their principals. In 1928, only 38% of elementary school principals were provided with full-time clerks, but 45% of the principals in larger cities reported having full-time assistance. On the average, superintendents assigned one school clerk for every 785 students.

As the principalship evolved into a distinctive role, separate and superordinate to that of teachers, the demographic characteristics of the profession were also changing. In 1923, Cubberly, in his book *The Principal and His School*, assigned the school leadership role to males, but there were actually more females (55%) than males in the principal's position at the time. That proportion marked an all-time high for females in that role in the United States. It was followed by a decline in the number of female principals, continuous until recently. That proportion was 18% in 1978 and has now risen to 20% (Doud, 1988) Thus, as the prestige of the principal's role increased, male dominance of these positions also increased.

According to Adkinson (1981), the professionalization of educational administration served to differentiate administrators from teachers by emphasizing the "masculine" concerns of management rather than the "feminine" concerns of nurturance and instruction. As described by Whitney (1926), "the elementary school principal will become the most important school official. . . .His office should be scientifically developed. . . .He will be the expert supervisor, the expert technician. . . .He should be given large powers within his own school and held accountable."

In order to accomplish this, superintendents were urged to conceive of each school as a unit under a trained supervising principal furnished with "nontechnical help from clerks" (National Education Association, 1928). As a result, the many tasks that these higher status principals deemed unworthy of their time were assigned to females. Although many of these women were college educated, they were assigned the devalued routines of the school office.

By 1929 there was a Clerical Assistants Association in Philadelphia. In 1930, clerical assistance in the elementary schools was so well entrenched that McClure, the first president of the Department of Elementary School Principals (DESP), was warning principals about losing their perspective as a result of too much reliance on their clerks.

Who were these clerks? What was their preparation for this position?

School Secretaries—The Early Years

The Bulletin of the National Association of School Secretaries (the NASS was the precursor of the current National Association of Educational Office Personnel or NAEOP) is a major source of information about the early development of school secretaries. The first volume of *The National Secretary* was published in 1936. It was introduced by Louise Henderson, president of the NASS and was prefaced by "A Message of Encouragement" from Willard E. Givens, then executive secretary of the National Education Association (NEA). Givens noted the importance of the school secretary as "a source of helpful and valuable information." He also argued that a large part of the responsibility for a smoothly running school system rested on the school secretary (Givens, 1936).

Henderson's message was also encouraging. The 1936 goal for the fledgling organization was the publication of a national bulletin "to stimulate interest, to promote exposure and closer contact." She proudly announced membership of 600 secretaries in 34 states, and the recent adoption of a constitution and by-laws. She also reminded members to pay their $1 dues promptly (Henderson, 1936).

These early years of NASS were characterized, as evidenced in *The National Secretary*, by concerns for professionalization, recognition and the tendency to associate with educators rather than with other clerical and secretarial workers. Fellowship was also emphasized, and the triannual bulletin was seen as a vehicle to improve communication among school secretaries.

In their search for recognition, the secretaries turned to the leadership of the NEA as well as to national spokespersons in education. Most early issues of *The National Secretary* included a brief message from a notable educator. These messages were always encouraging and full of praise for the work done by school secretaries. Charles B. Glenn, for example, the 1937 president of the American Association of School Administrators, noted how "[school secretaries] bear an important part of the responsibility of creating for the administration a favorable impression on the public. . . .." And in 1938 Emerson H. Landis, school superintendent of Dayton, Ohio, pointed to the school secretary's "unique" position and her service in "training pupils."

A recurrent theme, both from the NASS leadership and the established educators who wrote in the bulletin, was the need to raise standards. Henderson, who as the first president guided the NASS through its formative stages, was a strong advocate of state certification for school secretaries. She called on local, state, and national organizations to work on "rigid entrance requirements," including "an intensive period of training equal to that of a teacher." Through these measures, Henderson expected to gain better salaries as well as tenure and retirement privileges for the secretaries (Henderson, 1937), goals that are yet to be attained.

Early confounding of teachers and school secretaries is not surprising because substitute teachers were employed as school secretaries in the early years. The biography of Margaret Kernan, first chairperson of the Publications Committee, and later vice-president of the NASS, mentioned her then-recent presidency of the Salem City Teachers' Club, and membership in the Executive Committee of the New Jersey Association of Teacher Assistants to the Principal. President Henderson was also a member of the Philadelphia Teacher's Association (*The National Secretary*, 1937).

The relationship between the NASS and the educational community was enhanced through close coordination of their meetings. It was not a one-way relationship. In 1937 the NEA conducted a survey on "Administrative Practices Affecting Clerical Employees in City School Systems." The NEA director of membership in 1937, T. D. Martin, considered school secretaries to be unqualifiedly eligible for membership in the Association since the by-laws stipulated active membership to be available "to anyone. . .engaged in the profession or other educational work" (Martin, 1937).

The openness of the NEA by-laws was put to the test when the NASS requested permission to become a department of the association. Early rumblings about affiliation with the NEA were given a concrete form in May 1941 when a committee of the NASS was appointed to conduct research on the possibility of establishing a direct relationship with the NEA.

An encouraging report from this committee led to a formal application for departmental status for the NASS. In the summer of 1944 a committee met with the executive secretary of the NEA who suggested increasing the school secretary's membership in the NEA. He also recommended drafting a petition for NEA membership from at least 200 NASS members. Once these two steps were accomplished, the executive secretary would present a petition at the 1945 summer meeting of the NEA board of directors. The request would come to the Representative Assembly for approval a year later (*The National Secretary*, 1944).

Givens was true to his word. In a letter to the president of the NASS, he reported approval of the NASS request by the NEA board of directors. A year later the motion was carried by the Representative Assembly. The first departmental report of the NASS appeared among the NEA proceedings of 1946. The purposes of the NASS were listed: "To elevate the standards of the group and through organization, to pool ideas and ideals toward a fine and more efficient service to the school and community. The Association had a four-point program: service, information, recognition, and fellowship" (National Education Association, 1947).

Early Characteristics of the Work Force

The earliest data available on school clerks was reported in the Sixth Yearbook of the Department of Elementary School Principals (DESP) in 1926. They tell us that the main supplier of school clerks at that time was the "Commercial Department of High Schools" (42%). The "Civil Service" was second with 24%, but 15% of the supply pool was classified as "teachers, normal graduates, and college graduates." In 1926 the median minimum salary for elementary school clerks in cities with populations of more than 75,000 population was $735; the maximum was $1,265 (McGill, 1926). These figures compare with a median salary for urban-area elementary school teachers (cities with populations between 30,000 and 100,000) of $1,565 (NEA, 1926).

The Eighth Yearbook of the DESP published the results of a survey conducted by Louise Henderson (Henderson, 1929) on the clerical service available in city school systems. The questionnaire had been sent to 82 superintendents but only 38 answered. All answered affirmatively to the question of whether elementary schools were provided with clerical assistance. Almost half of the cities responding reported that high school training was required for the school clerical position. Almost one-third also required an examination, and a few required teaching experience.

Average school clerk salaries reported by cities responding to the survey ranged from a low of $985 to a high of $2,284 and averaged $1,635. These salaries, reported as annual, were probably 10 month salaries, and thus can be compared to those reported in the survey I conducted for this study in 1984. One city, New York, anchored the upper end of the continuum, reporting a low of $1,400 and a maximum of $5,000 for the clerk (Henderson, 1929).[2] Interestingly,

55 years later, one of the secretaries responding to the 1984 survey also reported a 10-month salary of $5,000. This suggests a dramatic devaluation of the secretary's work since 1929.

A comparison of the average salary for school secretaries in 1929 with the average salary for instructional staff, which was $1,420 in 1930 (Bureau of the Census, 1975)[3], suggests that school secretaries' salaries were better than that of teachers. Caution must be used, however, because in 1929 most of the secretaries were located in the larger urban districts that also offered the larger salaries to instructional staff. But the total instructional staff salaries used in this comparison would have included the smallest districts in the nation as well as the wealthier urban areas. The difference would skew the results in favor of the secretaries.

To correct that imbalance I compared the lower end of the secretaries' salaries to those of the instructional staff. In that case the secretaries' salaries equal almost 70% of the instructional staff's total average salary. In other words, the lowest school secretary salaries in 1929 were about 30% below the salaries for the combined instructional staff. That ratio is much more favorable than the ratio discovered through this study.

The average salary reported by secretaries responding to the survey for this book was $12,500, only 54% of the average salary reported for elementary school teachers that year, and 37% of the average salary reported for elementary school principals. Once again we must bear in mind that few of the respondents to this survey were located in the larger urban areas. The inclusion of those areas would be likely to improve the ratio; however, it would never reach the more favorable 70% ratio of 1929.

The following expectations for the school secretary were suggested in 1928 as appropriate for superintendents and elementary school principals to hold:

She can handle the supply room, deal with many pupil cases, get rid of callers the principal should not waste time on, answer the inquiries of many parents and make engagements for the principal with others, answer the telephone, reply to much of the mail, make and file records, fill our requisitions, compile many of the school reports, execute many directions from the principal as to work or people to call up and see, remind the principal of things to be done in case he forgets, and manage the office and answer inquiries in his absence. (National Education Association, 1928)

It should be noted that these expectations assign two conflicting roles to the school secretary. On the one hand, the secretary is assigned duties considered to be beneath the principal, supporting the assumption that the principal holds the power while the secretary plays a subservient role. On the other hand, the secretary is also expected to speak for the principal during his (sic) absence. Thus during selected periods she is expected to assume the power. This situation forces the secretary into what I call position of "intermittent power." Intermittent power requires the subordinate to control any tendencies to assume responsibility while in the presence of the superordinate, and yet be ready to assume the very same responsibilities during the superordinate's absence.

A position of intermittent power requires exquisite balancing, a skill with which women are well acquainted. It resembles traditional marital relationships where mother is expected to be powerful as long as father is unavailable and his patriarchal position of power is not threatened. It is the position against which Nora rebelled in Ibsen's *A Doll's House,* and its consequences were played out by thousands of women who were dismissed from the factories and returned to home and hearth during the post-WWII period. Intermittent power is inherent in the relationships between physicians and nurses at countless hospitals as well as in many other positions traditionally held by females. Power for these women is not a constant quality of their jobs. It is instead subject to the vagaries of the superordinate's presence who is, most often, a male.

It is interesting that the writer of the expectations for school secretaries (NEA, 1928) assumes a male principal and a female secretary although the majority of the nation's school principals were female at that time and clerical positions were still rather new. It may be that only a female traditionally socialized to accept ambiguity in her relationships would have been expected to tolerate the position described.

The anonymous quote delineating expectations of school secretaries (NEA, 1928) also foretold in its genderized nouns the coming decline in female school leaders and the increasing male dominance of the role. This decline was probably due to the increased emphasis on the managerial rather than the instructional role of the principal. Women who were also teachers were apparently able to convince decision makers of their instructional competence and thereby assume the combined teacher/leader role. They lost those positions when the role was redefined as a strictly managerial one. Thus as the size and complexity of the schools changed so did the principalship, which became a male prerogative. It was also during this time that the position of school secretary became institutionalized. A possible connection between these parallel changes will be explored in a later chapter.

Current Perceptions

The history of the school secretary's role reveals a job description closely allied to teachers as well as to principals. Historical accounts suggest that, in the early years, school secretaries were more apt to be considered important contributors to the educational endeavor. Such recognition is scarce in the current educational scene. Evidence is found in the textbooks used in training educational leaders. Such books would be expected to cover areas considered to be important in the adequate preparation of potential administrators.

Following this assumption, I examined textbooks used in courses designed for the training of school leaders. Nine textbooks were selected after consultation with several professors of educational administration. The selection was based on the texts' frequency of use, and did not entail judgments of relative value. The sample includes all those books currently considered to be standards in the field, however: Blumberg and Greenfield (1980); Campbell, Corbally, and Nystrand (1983); Drake and Roe (1986); Hoy and Miskel (1987); Kimbrough and Burkett (1990); Knezevich (1984); Lipham, Rankin, and Hoeh (1985); Saxe (1980); Ubben and Hughes (1989).

The purpose of the analysis was to find out what, if anything, these textbooks might have to say about the school office and about the school's clerical support. In each case the table of contents and the index were examined for mentions of the terms secretary, clerical help, or the school office. When appropriate, sections on community or public relations were also examined with the expectation that popular wisdom about the secretary's role—"the public face of the school"—might be reflected there.

The Secretary in the Textbooks

In Knezevich's book (1984), for example, the public relations section covers several pages where he discusses the problem of getting information to the public. He notes the important role teachers play in fostering school-community relations, yet he never mentions the daily interactions that take place in the school office. Kimbrough and Burkett (1990) advise the principal on the importance of first impressions for visitors to the school, but they also ignore the contribution of the secretary, the person who is most visible and available in the school office.

Ubben and Hughes (1989) make a passing reference to the secretary in a brief section on classified personnel, but they give more attention to the custodian. Nonetheless, they point out that technical competence should not be the only standard by which classified personnel are judged. In a school, they argue, competence must include the realization that most of these personnel will be working with children and must, therefore, have a proper attitude toward, and understanding of, young people.

The most extensive section on the school secretary appears in Drake and Roe (1986). These authors devote a whole chapter to the school office, and a section within the chapter to the secretary. They call the office "the communication, information, and production center for the school," and name the secretary "the voice of the school" (p. 393). The importance of the secretary's role in setting the tone for the school through her pleasant demeanor and willingness to help is emphasized by these authors.

It is interesting that the two textbooks that do mention the secretary are all oriented to the practice rather than the theory of educational administration.

Books with a heavy theoretical orientation, such as Campbell, Corbally, and Nystrand (1983) or Hoy and Miskel (1987), make no mention of the school secretary, although they assign several pages to communication processes. Campbell et al., for example, note how it is important for the administrator to develop "feelings" channels of communication in order to be aware of how things look "on the front lines." Hoy and Miskel point out how the grapevine, as an informal communication channel, can be an important device in the implementation of organizational objectives. In their failure to acknowledge the secretary as a key person in informal channels of communication, these authors seem to ignore their own theories.

The neglect, in this set of workbooks, of the person to whom school folklore assigns the actual running of the school is surprising. Why this should be so is a matter of speculation beyond the reach of my study. Suffice it to say that the near absence of the school secretary from these academic sources is bound to suggest to aspiring school administrators that neither the school office nor the people who work in it will be very important to their work. This message runs counter to conventional wisdom and also to the reality they will encounter as soon as they assume leadership positions in the schools.

NOTES

1. The label applied to what Henderson (1929) called "school helpers" has changed through the years and continues to vary. In a 1929 survey Henderson found that half of the 30 cities responding used the term secretary to designate these employees, another 13 used the term clerk or clerical assistant, and two referred to them as stenographers. For the sake of consistency I will use secretary throughout this work, although those responding to the survey reported in this book were also variously labeled by their districts. One of the respondents noted that her district insisted on using the term clerical help in order to downgrade the position.

2. While the reference simply mentions an annual salary, it was generally paid to cover a 10-month period.

3. The category termed instructional staff included, at that time, supervisors of instruction, principals, teachers, guidance personnel, librarians, and psychological personnel. (Bureau of the Census, 1975). This aggregation was probably necessary due to the lack of clear lines of demarcation between those positions. Figures for 1929 are not included in the table from this source, so 1930 is used as the comparison year.

TWO

Who Are the School Secretaries?

UNDERSTANDING THE ROLE

A study such as this one is typically preceded by a literature review providing a structure of existing knowledge into which the new knowledge derived from the study can be incorporated. Without such an underlying framework, research findings, while interesting in themselves, may remain isolated and the sought-for understanding will remain elusive. In the case of this study, the task was made difficult by the dearth of literature on elementary school secretaries.

Research related to the school secretary tends to be focused on her relationship with the principal or teachers, rather than on her work. The unpublished dissertations of Russell (1973) and Jackson (1976) are of this type. Others have attempted to understand the motivation (Simon, 1972) and training needs (Church, 1971; Rahe, 1960) of that population. More recently Rimer (1984) published a paper describing research he was conducting at that time. And Hart (1985) reported on a study of secondary school secretaries in London. With the exception of Rimer and Hart, the research available on the topic fails to deal with the nature of the job. It would have been, therefore, rather unproductive to limit this review to that existing body of knowledge. It was necessary to devise other means to facilitate understanding the school secretary's role.

Fortunately, the breadth of the school secretary's job lends itself to a framework constructed of three research perspectives, each of

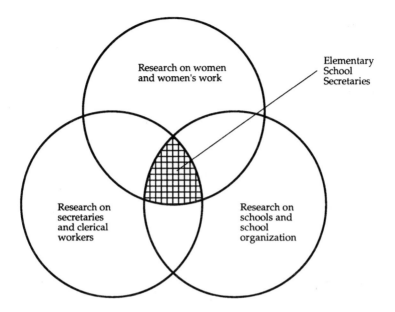

Figure 2.1 Framework for the Literature Review

which contributes particular insights to an understanding of the role of the elementary school secretary. These three perspectives are not discrete, they overlap (see Figure 2.1) and in their conjunction may be found the closest approximation to a knowledge base that can serve as a framework for the study reported here. The three overlapping perspectives are derived from three characteristics of the position.

The first characteristic encompasses the feminine character of this population. Almost all school secretaries are female. Although a few males have recently entered their ranks, they still constitute only a tiny minority of the total. As females, school secretaries constitute a subgroup within the much larger population of females. They share with the universe of females a number of characteristics that can influence their view of the world and their position in it. Gender-related research documents women's experiences and world views. It is a comparatively young field, but it has already produced a voluminous literature. It is not possible to review all of that literature here. Only selected portions that contribute to an understanding of female behavior, particularly in work settings, and specifically in white-collar positions are presented.

The second characteristic of elementary school secretaries is that they are secretaries. They perform many functions closely related to those performed by the much larger group of secretaries. While research on secretaries is by no means plentiful, a few studies can contribute to an understanding of that position, and that literature is reviewed here.

Last, a set of cultural characteristics attends the position of elementary school secretaries. Schools are cultural settings where people interact in particular ways. The behavior of the elementary school secretary is at least partly contingent on the setting in which she works. The culture of the school has been examined for many years by many people. Only a part of this extensive literature is explored here, limited to that which facilitates gaining a better understanding of the setting where school secretaries work.

The review begins with the cultural context, the broadest of these research perspectives. The focus then shifts to gender-related research, and then to the research on secretaries in general. The section ends with a summary integrating these three perspectives and with conclusions derived from the scarce research data available on the subject of elementary school secretaries.

The School Setting

Comparisons between the school secretary's work and the work of other secretaries reflect the public tendency to compare schools to business settings. Such comparisons have dominated research on schools as organizations for many years.

During the early years of the twentieth century, the cult of efficiency prevailed and "experts" tended to equate schools as workplaces with business establishments. Organizational theories were borrowed from the corporate world and fitted to, often imposed upon, the school. Schedules, time management, and efficiency were all grafted onto the educational endeavor. When the school failed to behave in accordance with the theory, it was assumed that something was wrong with the school.

More recently, theorists have been questioning this view. Many have suggested alternative models. Some have argued that, while the classical, business-model administrator acts on the basis of knowledge about the objectives of the organization, technology, and past experience, all three of these sources are ambiguous in education. They have suggested an alternative model of schools as "organized anarchies," that is, "organizations in which technologies are unclear, goals ambiguous and participation fluid" (March, 1974; March & Olsen, 1976).

Hanson (1984) finds discrepancies in the metaphors used by theorists to explain the schools and those used by practitioners in the schools. She argues that research on schools as organizations is bound by mechanistic, impersonal metaphors that constrain our view of schooling. Hanson suggests the need for an alternative paradigm that can bring to the fore the human aspects of schooling.

Sergiovanni (1984) proposed an alternative paradigm of leadership as cultural expression and of organizations as multicultural societies. The goal in such societies is to build a "cultural federation of compatibility that provides enough common identity, enough common meanings, and enough of a basis for committed action for the organization to function in spirited concert" (p. 107).

In a like vein, Deal (1985) noted the similarity in public dissatisfaction with business and schools, and the usefulness for the schools of the emerging "softer, people-oriented, symbolic strategy" characteristic of successful companies (p. 605). According to Deal, culture, in everyday usage, may be stated as "the way we do things around here" and consists of patterns of thought, behavior, and artifacts that symbolize and give meaning to the workplace.

These examples suggest a trend away from the rational business model toward a model that more closely reflects the human, rather than the abstract institutional, aspects of schools. This trend has been fueled by a body of qualitative research about schools, which has highlighted the unique characteristics of the setting, its human element, and its ambiguities (Wolcott, 1973; Morris, Crowson, Hurwitz, & Porter-Gehrie, 1981; Hannay & Stevens, 1984; Feirsen, 1989). However, such research has either focused on the classroom or on the principal. Very little attention has been given to the secretary's work in the school office or to the effect of that work on the school's operation. But hints to that effect may be found in the literature reporting research on principals and effective schools.

Contributions to school effectiveness

A review of 39 studies of the elementary school principal (Leithwood & Montgomery, 1982) reveals that effective principals differed from typical principals in their attention to procedures, organizational arrangements, allocation of out-of-classroom materials, and physical resources. In addition, effective principals resisted the pressure of "administrivia" by establishing efficient procedures for handling routines. And in a 1981 survey conducted by the National Association of Secondary School Principals, those principals reputed to be effective listed an efficient secretary as one of their important assets (Pharis, 1981).

Hawley, Rosenholtz, Goodstein, and Hasselbring (1984) also found evidence in the literature that effective principals attended to the material requirements and organization of instructional programs; provided clerical assistance for routine paperwork and unnecessary tasks; and mobilized outside resources to assist teachers with routine, nonteaching tasks.

In an intensive study of one specific principal, Hannay and Stevens (1984) focused on the connection between the principal's managerial work and the effectiveness of the school as a learning environment. They found that the principal exerted indirect influence on the curriculum (defined as the experiences children have in schools) by taking action through managerial tasks with the intention of influencing the curriculum.

Similarly Barr, Dreeben, and Wiratachi (1983) have argued that the principal's influence on learning stems less from the much-discussed area of leadership than from inconspicuous events related to the allocation of resources to classes. They further state that some of these activities have been designated as clerical chores. And Rutter et al. (1979) found that the more successful schools were likely to be seen by teachers as providing them with adequate clerical support.

Further evidence for the potential contribution of the secretary to school effectiveness can be found in a school improvement program carried out in Washington (Hager & Scarr, 1983). Cognizant of the new and complex issues facing principals, Lake Washington School District 414 undertook an evaluation and assessment of the administrative structure at the building level. Their findings revealed that elementary school secretaries were involved in so many legitimate office activities that they were only available to principals about 10% of the time. Principals had, therefore, been forced to assume additional responsibility for office activities. As a result of this investigation, each elementary school principal was allocated an additional half-time secretary. This was only one among several modifications in the district's administrative structure that the authors credit for significant, positive improvement in the schools.

It appears, therefore, that "administrivia" may not be so trivial. A principal's ability to handle the routine activities of school operation may have important consequences for the instructional program and for the principal's general effectiveness. But the principal is not alone in the school office. Yet to be understood is the part that school secretaries may play in the performance of clerical chores and other functions that may be related to a school's effectiveness.

Women's Work

In 1975 more than two fifths of all women workers were employed in 10 occupations: secretary, retail trade sales, bookkeeper, private household worker, elementary school teacher, waitress, typist, sewer and stitcher, cashier, and registered nurse. Each of these occupations employed more than 800,000 people (U.S. Department of Labor, 1975). The total for these 10 occupations constituted close to half of the total female labor force in that year. At the same time, male employment was much less concentrated within specific job categories. These figures constitute an increased concentration of female labor in certain jobs through the years, particularly in clerical jobs. Females in that classification have increased, as a proportion of all employed women, from 21.6% in 1940 to 35% in 1979. By 1979, females constituted 98.2% of all clerical workers (Bureau of the Census, 1985).

Lopata, Miller, and Barnewolt (1984) ascribe the lopsidedness of women's participation in the labor force, at least in part, to the failure of the system to make adjustments in the rhythm of work to accommodate those (primarily female) who face role conflict due to family responsibilities. They believe that one reason for this lack of flexibility is that "society still does not approve of paid employment outside of the home for mothers" (p. 58). Thus, they argue, women are channeled into work that is compatible with their domestic responsibilities.

Tepperman (1976) points out the ambiguity inherent in public perceptions that office work is both privileged and unimportant. She has sought to encourage women to organize and demand concrete rewards for their work. She argues that myths about office work, such as "we're like one big happy family here," are intended to appeal to women and keep them satisfied with their lot.

In spite of the large numbers of clerical workers and the many complaints they voice, unionization of this group has been difficult. According to Kanter (1977), this may be partly due to the association between a secretary's status and that of her boss, which demands that she develop a close relationship to that boss if she wants to advance at all.

Another explanation may be that women may focus much more on their families than do men, and may therefore be less willing to invest time and energy into improving their jobs. Studies of job satisfaction have suggested that women's job satisfaction may be influenced more by hygiene than motivator factors. Hygiene factors include a good boss and good physical working conditions, as well as salary, job security, and fringe benefits. Motivator factors include challenge, advancement, and decision making (Williamson & Karras, 1970). But Lopata et al. (1984) counter that women's emphasis on the social aspects of their jobs is understandable given the lack of challenge and mobility of their positions.

An important and highly controversial work of gender-related research was published by Gilligan in 1982. She argued that male researchers had applied a narrow focus to their activities and had then proceeded to generalize their findings across social groupings. She was concerned with the exclusion of women from the critical, theory-building studies of psychological research. In her research Gilligan found evidence that women's moral development centers on the elaboration of intimacy, relationships and care. This line of development, she argued, is in contrast to that followed by males, which is directed toward the achievement of autonomy and responsibility. Adulthood and maturity have, unfortunately, come to be identified with male development, according to Gilligan. In that context women's concerns with relationships appear as a weakness and as a sign of immaturity. Gilligan uses this general framework to critique accepted psychological theories such as those of Freud, Piaget, Kohlberg, and Maslow.

Gilligan's psychological theorizing provides a counterpoint to the previously cited sociological work. The acceptance of Gilligan's view that women's patterns of development lead to an emphasis on relationships and caring requires rejection or modification of the sociological view with its emphasis on the structural characteristics of positions as major determinants of whether or not a job may be rewarding. That is, if as Gilligan claims, women "order human experience in terms of different priorities" (p. 22), then it is to be expected that: (a) they gravitate toward jobs that fulfill those priorities, and (b) that they would, in any job, devote more attention to those functions that tend to fulfill those priorities. If Gilligan is right, then the problems of women in the workplace may be less related to structural problems, and more related to social exploitation. These issues are at the heart of current debates about the "proper" place of women in the world of work and underlie this study.

Secretaries' Work

Elementary school secretaries are generally females who work in school offices. In that setting they perform work that is in many ways similar to that of the multitude of women discussed above. Secretaries as a group have not been of much interest to researchers, even though they comprise 19% of the total workforce, a proportion that was projected to rise to 27% by 1990 (U.S. Department of Labor Statistics, 1983). There are two particularly helpful studies of secretaries in business settings and one of secretaries for a state mental facility, however, which can contribute to our understanding of the secretary's role and provide a baseline against which to compare the work of school secretaries.

The first, conducted by Vinnicombe (1980), is a study of secretaries in organizations. It focuses directly on the secretary's role in the office and on the boss-secretary interaction. The second study, conducted by Kanter (1977), is primarily a study of an organization where the interactions across levels and roles, as well as between male and female behavior in the organization, are highlighted. The third study by Evans (1987) is an ethnographic study intended to describe the clerical workers' perspective of their work lives.

Secretaries in the business office

Vinnicombe's study is one of the few thorough analyses of the secretarial role. She views the secretarial role as a continuum beginning with the pool typist, whose job is purely mechanistic, to the senior executive secretary, who spends little or no time typing and may even have her own junior secretary. At this upper level, the secretary spends most of her day in a supportive, administrative capacity carrying out a variety of tasks. Thus, according to Vinnicombe, the term secretary encompasses a large variety of roles with varying degrees of responsibility.

Further variation in role occurs, says Vinnicombe, as a function of the different settings where the secretary performs her duties. The size of the organization and whether it is a top executive's office or that of a middle manager will affect the secretary's role. We would therefore expect the unique characteristics of a school to also modify the secretary's role.

Vinnicombe conducted five in-depth interviews with private secretaries. One of them worked for a department head in a university. That secretary's description of her job differed from the descriptions offered by the other four secretaries interviewed, all of whom worked in business offices. She said the largest portion of her day was spent in dealing with constant interruptions. She also noted the importance of personal relationships to her work. It is interesting that, although this secretary was working in a university setting, the two characteristics that distinguished her work from that of the business secretaries were also cited by the elementary school secretaries in this study.

Secretaries in the organization

Kanter's (1977) study takes a broader perspective, but our interest here is in what she had to say about the organization's secretaries. Her study focused on all the people who work in the corporate offices of one organization. This population included everyone from the top executive and managers to what she calls the "corps of paper-handlers, recordkeepers, and data manipulators" (p. 4) who occupy a physically contiguous space but in status are distant from the top of the hierarchy. Her focus was on individuals and their work experience.

According to Kanter, the several thousand secretaries in the corporation she studied typically moved through a typing pool where they had no permanent assignment, then to a situation where they were accountable to more than one boss. Finally after several years of experience, they worked for only one boss. At this level and beyond, promotions were tied to the recommendations of their bosses. Ultimately some of these women might advance to an executive secretarial position akin to the senior executive secretary described by Vinnicombe.

At the level where secretaries achieved a one-to-one relationship with their boss, Kanter found that the absence of job descriptions allowed bosses to determine what secretaries did and how they spent their time. The job was also characterized by a "constant flow of orders," which differentiated it from jobs in other parts of the bureaucracy where routines and schedules prevailed. The secretarial job was likely to be guided only by the general skeleton of a set of procedures for handling routines, and was always subject to the continuous modification of special requests and instructions.

Another way in which secretaries provided a personal service to their bosses was "as critical ingredients in their bosses presentation of a 'front' " (Kanter, 1977, p. 80). Secretaries participated in the behind-the-scenes transformation of chaos into order, they knew how their bosses really spent their time, and served as a buffer between their bosses and the rest of the world.

Secretaries in a public institution

Evans' (1987) study is most similar to the study reported here. Although the setting seems quite different, both schools and state mental institutions are publicly funded, multilayered settings. She found that departmental secretaries at this institution had multiple roles, one described by the formal system and another forced upon them by the need to act as buffer between the upper administration and the clinical personnel. Evans describes the formal organizational structure as composed of two factions: the Medical Records Department charged with the maintenance of statistics and records processing, and the professionally oriented clinical personnel. The missing link between them was filled by the department secretaries. They bridged the gap between the rigid demands for accountability of the state mental health system and the hands-on, interpersonal tasks of the clinical personnel. The service performed by these women, though unacknowledged by the organization, was critical for its survival.

Secretaries in the schools

As has been noted before, research on school secretaries is scarce. Saxe (1968) notes that one might expect to find much research devoted to a job requiring such a wide range of competencies; however, this is not the case. He suggests that the lack of critical analysis may be due to a general lack of appreciation of the secretary's role.

One of the more comprehensive works is a review of the literature by Stowell (1974). He found an acknowledgment of the value and administrative input of the school secretary in the 1950s and references to secretaries as "indispensable," "an extension of the principal," and in a comprehensive description, " part office worker, part administrator's right hand, part mother-away-from-home and part public relations officer" during the sixties (p. 42). There were also, at that time, rumblings of role conflict between principals and secretaries. These conflicts were supposed to be more frequent in small school districts where, it was said, the secretary had a tendency to act as an administrative assistant.

A 1970 study by Ford, cited by Stowell (1974), found that principals and secretaries held conflicting ideas of the secretary's responsibilities. The secretaries reported accepting greater responsibility for tasks than was indicated by their principals. Three years later in a similar study that included teachers, Russell (1973) found differences in both the role expectations and perceptions of actual performance held by teachers, principals, and secretaries. Russell concluded that the elementary school secretary occupied a position of potentially high conflict.

In a different vein, Simon (1972) completed a study of the motivating factors for both elementary and secondary school secretaries. He found that this occupation "attracts and retains persons who enjoy human interaction, working with children, and associating with other people" (p. 111). He also found them to be more similar to teachers than to professionals in industry regarding the aspects of the job that motivate them. Last, he found that salary was completely negligible as a satisfier and relatively unimportant as a dissatisfier.

More recently, Rimer (1984) conducted an ethnographic study of three elementary school secretaries. He found that the position "not only requires a multitude of duties and skills, but also demands organization, time management, self-motivation and discretion" (p. 18). He concluded that the elementary school secretary was an indispensable member of the school staff and should be recognized as such.

Sweeney (1987), after interviewing secretaries and their principals, found that those who had established from the beginning a mutually satisfying process of communication, tended to continue that pattern and enjoyed good working relationships. Sweeney also found that the secretaries gave a great deal of importance to the principal's support, and that the school secretary's job was not static. She advised principals to keep an open mind and to transfer some of their tasks to the school secretary. Doing so, she argued, would free the principal from some desk duties, as well as provide job enrichment for the secretaries.

Hart (1985) also found reason to suggest that heads (principals) of secondary schools transfer some of their responsibilities to their secretaries. He also described six aspects of the secretary's job as: (a) substitute parent, (b) the eyes and ears of the head, (c) sounding board, (d) the leader of the school support staff, (e) gatekeeper, and (f) financial consultant.

Thus the literature available on school secretaries suggests similarities between their jobs and those of their counterparts in other settings. In general, the secretarial role appears to be fluid, varied, and subject to contextual differences and to the interdependence of the boss/secretary relationship. A major difference for the school secretaries lies in the multilayered characteristic of schools, which demands service to a variety of clients, all intimately connected to the secretary. This environment appears to increase the opportunities for discrepancies in role expectations and, therefore, the possibilities for conflict. This problem will be discussed in a later section.

OVERVIEW OF THIS STUDY

This study is based on qualitative, quantitative, and archival data collected during the 1984-1985 academic year. The qualitative data consists of observations at six elementary school sites, and interviews with those six secretaries and their principals. Quantitative data was collected through a national survey of 297 elementary school secretaries. Archival data consists of content analysis of official documents represented by 27 job descriptions and nine textbooks of educational administration. The latter analysis was updated to include the latest editions of books reviewed earlier, and newly published books. Details about methods and instruments used may be found in Appendix A.

The next section relies on findings from the survey to describe the women who work in elementary school offices.

DEMOGRAPHIC CHARACTERISTICS

Who works as a school secretary? What kinds of training and experiences do they bring to the job? Why do they choose these positions? Many of the items in the survey were meant to answer such questions. I have used the secretaries' responses to these questions to construct a comprehensive portrait of the women who work as elementary school secretaries.

The Elementary School Secretary: A Composite

The typical elementary school secretary, according to these self-reported data, is female, about 52, married and has 2 to 3 children who are no longer living at home. She works in the same district where she lives and her children probably attended the school where she now works. She is also white, a monolingual English-speaker, and in excellent health.

This composite secretary is a high school graduate and has taken business courses. She was probably briefly employed before getting married and becoming a parent. She stayed home with her young children, and through the years she volunteered at the local school and probably taught Sunday School. When her children were older she tried to find a paying job that would be compatible with their school schedule and where her business training and experience would be useful.

All these needs were met by the elementary school office. She knew that the pay was low and there was no chance for advancement, but she was working mainly for the stimulation and to provide a few dollars for "extras." She started the job with little more training than that acquired in business school. She found that her years of experience as a volunteer, however, were helpful to her in the new position. This typical secretary has now been with the same district for about 15 years and has worked for almost 12 years in the same school. She has been there longer than the current principal with whom she has worked for about 6 years.

Her salary, as she expected, remains low. She earns about $12,500 (1985) for 10 months' work. She knows it is only about one third of what the principal earns and she wishes it were better. Though she is happy in her job and finds much appreciation among her co-workers in the school, she would like monetary recognition for what she is doing.

This typical elementary school secretary works by herself in her office and answers to a male principal. For a few hours every week a nurse and sometimes a counselor occupy nearby offices. She thinks highly of her principal and believes she is most helpful to him in maintaining records, providing support, and providing information. Among her routine tasks the elementary school secretary counts record keeping, correspondence, answering the telephone, and providing first aid. She is usually responsible for the staff bulletin, parents' newsletter, and the administrator's paperwork. Because she keeps the books for all accounts and the many small accounts in the school add up to a few thousand dollars a year, this typical secretary also does a lot of bookkeeping.

The typical secretary enjoys her work, particularly its variety. She likes working with many different people and finds it difficult to establish priorities among them. If forced to choose she would probably say that she most enjoys working with the students, but she also recognizes that the administrator's work must take priority.

Professional activities for this typical respondent include regular meetings with her colleagues, participation in her local association chapter, and many years of membership in the National Association of Elementary Office Personnel. She enjoys the group's publications and workshops, but she would like the association to help elementary school secretaries to gain proper recognition. She hopes such recognition would also help to raise their salaries.

How School Secretaries Compare

The elementary school secretaries who answered the survey differ from the total female labor force in several ways. They are older (average age of 52 compared to 44 for the total female labor force), more likely to be married (86% compared to 53%) (Bureau of the Census, 1985). In addition, fully 83% of the secretaries responding lived in the same district in which they worked, 41% worked in their neighborhood schools, and the children of 47% of the respondents attended (or had once attended) the same school. Two grandmothers also indicated that their grandchildren were now attending the same school.

This sample of secretaries also reported more formal schooling than the average female of their age in the country (only 29% of females 25 years or older had completed high school in 1960, compared to 80% of the secretaries responding to the survey). This achievement also places them above average when compared to other females in their work classification (technical/sales/administrative). In 1984 the proportion of this group that had completed high school was 56% (Bureau of the Census, 1985).

Minorities were underrepresented among the secretaries responding to the survey. Very few of the respondents classified themselves as Afro-American (4%, 12 cases) or Hispanic (2%, 7 cases), and none classified themselves as American Indian or Oriental. Not surprisingly, 92.5% of those responding classified themselves as monolingual speakers of English. Most of them also reported working in schools where the majority of the student population was Anglo-American. These results reflect the lower response to the survey from urban areas.

Training and Experience

Training for most school secretaries does not often extend beyond their K-12 schooling and shorthand, that traditional symbol of secretarial work, which is apparently disappearing quickly from the school office. Almost one half of the secretaries surveyed (45%) reported they could not take shorthand and almost three fourths (74.7%) said they did not use it in their work. Most secretaries (79%) reported that their districts did not require the skill as a condition for employment but one of the two districts included in this study did require that skill. Only one among the six principals in the two districts, however, expected the school secretary to use shorthand to take dictation.

Almost two thirds of the secretaries responding to the survey had received no training at all for the job and only one fourth reported receiving such training after hiring, most often through self-initiated efforts. Child development and cross-cultural understanding were most often mentioned by the school secretaries as areas where they needed training.

The respondents as a group reported many years of experience in and out of the elementary schools; most reported five and one-half years of secretarial experience outside of the school setting. Only one quarter of the secretaries reported no experience outside of the schools. On average, they had been employed in elementary schools for 15 years; a few reported as many as 22 years of service.

Most of the secretaries reported experience as school volunteers and Sunday School teachers as useful preparation for the positions they now held. Many of them added mother, scout leadership, and leadership in parent-teacher groups as additional worthwhile experience.

The secretaries interviewed for this study were very similar to the typical secretary described earlier. Their average age was 46 years old, and they were all married and had from one to three children. None of them had received training for the position, but all were high school graduates and most had received some business training. Three of them had also worked in business offices.

They had chosen the job mostly for the convenience of the schedule and because they enjoyed working with people, especially children. All of them said they were happy with their choice, in spite of the low pay.

The altruism suggested by the survey respondents' participation in volunteer activities was also evident among the interviewed secretaries. Not only had all of them been either school or church volunteers, most had also provided home care for an ailing parent for several years.

Given these characteristics of the women who are elementary school secretaries, what is that job like for them? To answer that question, I spent many hours observing the secretaries' activities in six elementary school offices.

SETTING THE CONTEXT

Among the various methods used in collecting data for this study, the six case studies were the most time consuming, as well as the most revealing. Many hours of observation in the six school offices, and lengthy interviews of the six secretaries and their respective principals constituted the bulk of the data for the case studies. They are also the backbone of this chapter, although relevant data from the survey has also been incorporated here. The goal is to gain as deep an understanding of the secretaries' work, attitudes, and concerns as possible.

The following brief descriptions of each of the six school sites and the people who worked there will provide a context for the data that follow.

Washington School

Washington School was only one year old. It housed 11 teachers (plus assorted support staff) and more than 250 students, most of

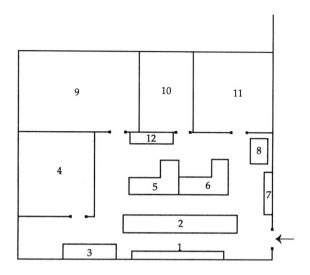

Legend:

1. Waiting area
2. Counter
3. Filing cabinets
4. Nurse's office
5. Secretary's desk
6. Attendance clerk's desk
7. Mailboxes
8. Photocopier
9. Principal's office
10. Counselor's office
11. Teacher's workroom
12. Filing cabinets

Figure 2.2 Washington School Office Plan

whom were classified as white (75%). The remaining student body consisted of 23% Mexican American and 2% American Indian. A 52% mobility ratio suggests this was not an altogether stable area.[1]

The small office at Washington School (see Figure 2.2) was divided by a high counter that separated a seating/waiting area from the secretary's and attendance clerk's desks. There were several offices behind them, including that of Ms. George, the principal, and a workroom where teachers congregated before and after classes and during their breaks. The teachers' mailboxes were also nearby and the nurse's office was at the opposite end of this office complex.

The office walls were almost totally covered with certificates, greeting cards, and cartoons, several of which honored Diane Green, the school secretary. All of these mementoes were aesthetically displayed. The largest wall was completely covered by a large outline map of the United States.

Diane was a tall, slender, soft-spoken woman whose continuous eye contact while she listened suggested undivided attention. She smiled often, and dressed simply and neatly but comfortably. Her movements were always fluid, never abrupt, giving an appearance of calm even when she was very busy.

Dewey School

The situation at Dewey School was unusual. It was one among several schools in District 1 that had to be closed until extensive construction work was completed. The total group of students, teachers, support and administrative staff was moved to a large, modern church meeting hall. It was as good a situation as could be hoped for, but it was not the school.

The temporary site (see Figure 2.3) was built roughly as a rectangle within a rectangle. The outer rectangle had small classrooms and a few offices all the way around. The inner rectangle was a very large open area. The main entrance was wide and spacious, decorated with religious pictures and photographs of leading church members.

One of the available executive offices was used by the counselor; the other one was shared by the principal, Mr. John, and the secretary, Edna Brown. Edna was on the short and plump side although not fat. She dressed smartly, always wore heels and kept her hair neatly coiffed. She had large expressive eyes and smiled often and easily.

A folding table placed against the far wall served as "the office." At the church site the secretary did not have a desk or files to rely on. Questions often had to wait until someone went over to the school to get the information. There were only three telephones (each on a separate line), no copier and, for a while, not even a typewriter. Only a few supplies were brought along. The rest had

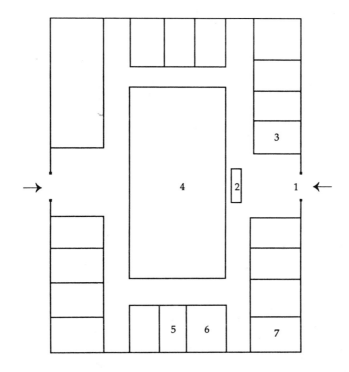

Legend:

1. Main entrance
2. Table set-up for office
3. Nurse's office
4. Primary area
5. Principal's office
6. Teachers' lounge
7. Counselor's office

Figure 2.3 Dewey School—Church Site Plan

to be fetched from the school. Since there were no mailboxes or a public announcement (p.a.) system, all communications had to be hand delivered.

The student population of Dewey School was 440, and 55% of these were minority students, mostly Mexican American. The school was located in a low-income area. Normally most of the children walked to school, but they were bused to the church.

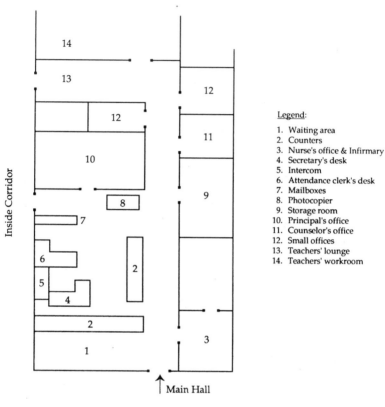

Figure 2.4 Fillmore School Office Plan

Fillmore School

Fillmore School was the largest school included in the sample. The student population was 818, moderately mobile (45%), and largely from the low socio-economic levels. Those classified as white comprised 57% of the school population. The next largest group was Mexican Americans at 35%. African Americans, American Indians, Orientals, and others made up the difference.

The staff consisted of 31 classroom teachers plus 32 other special and support staff. Mr. Millard was the principal of the school and Kathy Orange was the secretary.

The school building was large, open, modern, and only 5 years old. The school office was also spacious and open (see Figure 2.4).

A low counter separated the visitors' waiting area, furnished in simple institutional style, from the secretary's area. The nurse's office and a small infirmary were to the right immediately upon entering the office, and the principal's office was in the rear. The teachers' mailboxes were also in the back.

The office was decorated sparsely with several western landscapes, the school's logo, and pencils and t-shirts with the school name that were available for sale through the Parent Teacher Organization.

Kathy Orange was the youngest of the six secretaries observed. Of average height and weight, she dressed neatly but conservatively, smiled often, moved quickly, and was particularly adept at handling many things at once.

Grant School

Grant School had a student population of 707 composed of 60% white and 34% Mexican Americans. African Americans and American Indians made up the balance. The students were mostly from the lower middle class and were highly mobile (83%).

The staff at Grant School included 30 classroom teachers plus 18 special program personnel and support staff. Elsie Lavender was the secretary and Mr. Ulysses the principal.

The office at Grant School was quite small (see Figure 2.5). There was barely enough room for the secretary's and attendance clerk's desks. A five-foot-high counter separated the office area from the narrow entrance hall. Across from it were the nurse's office and a small infirmary. The photocopier was directly across from the secretary's desk. The principal's office was in the rear. A narrow hall led from his office to a work and storage area and the faculty lounge where the teachers' mailboxes were located.

The main office at Grant School had few decorations. Thematic, commercially produced cut-outs were placed around the bulletin boards. The bulletin boards were usually covered with schedules and notices, all in "ditto purple."

Elsie Lavender was in her mid-forties and very slender. She was witty and sometimes cutting in her remarks, which were laced with folk expressions. She usually dressed smartly and almost always wore high heels.

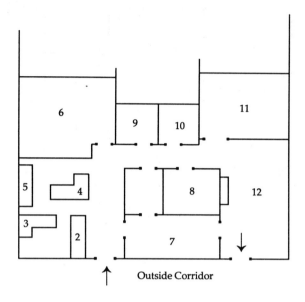

Legend:

1. Waiting area
2. Counter
3. Attendance clerk's desk
4. Secretary's desk
5. Intercom
6. Principal's office
7. Nurse's office & Infirmary
8. Counselor's office
9. Small office
10. Bathroom
11. Teachers' lounge
12. Teachers' workroom

Figure 2.5 Grant School Office Plan

Hayes School

Hayes School was a small school with 244 students and 11 classroom teachers. It was located near a university in a stable neighborhood. The mobility rate was only 25%.

The racial and ethnic composition of the student body was 66% white, 15% black, and 15% Mexican American. Three percent of the students were classified as American Indian and 1% as Oriental.

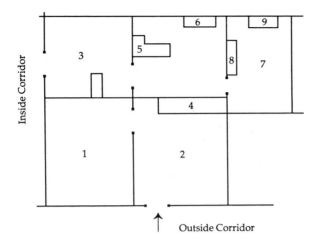

Legend:

1. Principal's office
2. Waiting area
3. Nurse's office & Infirmary
4. Counter
5. Secretary's desk
6. Intercom
7. Teachers' workroom
8. Mailboxes
9. Photocopier

Figure 2.6 Hayes School Office Plan

This was the first year at this school for Mr. Rutherford, the principal, and Sandy Pink, the secretary. They had worked together for 2 years at a larger school.

The 15-year-old building was much larger than required, and entire wings were given over to district offices. It was not a particularly attractive building—box-like and plain—but it was adjacent to a park, and the grounds were attractively kept.

The main office (see Figure 2.6) was not very large, but it was uncrowded. Visitors entered a waiting area that ended at a tall counter. The principal's office was to the left as one walked toward the secretary who sat facing the entrance. Her desk was placed

off-center so that the counter did not obstruct her view of the main
door. To her left was the intercom and to the right was an ample
nurse's office and infirmary. The walls around the office were
covered with attractive, sometimes "cute," commercially produced
posters with inspirational sayings on them.

Sandy Pink was in her late thirties, slim, and always attractively
dressed. She gave the appearance of being in motion all the time,
even when she was standing still. She smiled frequently and
always had cheerful words for people who passed by her desk.

Alvarez School

A large photograph of the couple after whom Alvarez School
was named was prominently displayed at the school's entrance
next to cabinets holding the school's logo and many trophies won
by the school's students or faculty. The building was almost 10
years old but had been well maintained and appeared newer. It was
a modern design, built around a central library/media center.

The school office (see Figure 2.7) was located to the right of the
main entrance and along a central corridor. The corridor led in one
direction to the cafeteria and in the other to the library. The corridor
was very wide and also served as a waiting area.

Only a low counter separated the main office area from the
corridor. The secretary's desk sat against the far wall and faced the
corridor when she typed. The principal's office was across from the
secretary and, in the back between both office areas, was the nurse's
office and a small infirmary.

The teachers' mailboxes were located near the secretary's desk.
Their workroom and lounge areas were on the other side of the
main entrance.

Ms. Alonso, the principal of Alvarez School, was assigned to this
school upon the unexpected resignation of her predecessor. The
opening day of the school year was also her first day as the school's
principal. The secretary, Mary Lime, was in her late forties, dressed
neatly and conservatively, wore sensible shoes, and was slightly
overweight. She had the appearance of a kindly, youthful grandmother. Her demeanor was always gentle and calm.

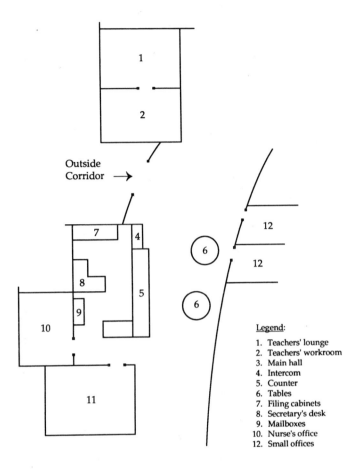

Figure 2.7 Alvarez School Office Plan

These six schools were the settings for the case studies conducted for this research. They differed in size and complexity, in student population served and in the length of the principal-secretary work relationship. They resembled each other in that they were all recommended by their respective school districts as "good" school offices where the secretary and the principal worked well together.

The next chapter describes the work that goes on in these offices.

NOTE

1. The mobility ratio, that is, the rate of turnover of each school, was computed by dividing the sum of the total number of entrants and the total number of transfers out during the 1984 school year by the 1985 October enrollment (1984 entrants + 1984 losses, divided by October 1985 enrollment).

THREE

The School Secretaries' World

The school secretaries' world is explored in this chapter, beginning with their workspace, continuing with the varied clientele they serve, and ending with their attitudes and concerns about the job.

The Secretary's Space

The school office is the secretary's space. What she needs in order to perform her work is contained in this area. This was made abundantly clear by Edna Brown's reaction to being away from the "office" due to repairs being made at Dewey School. She complained about missing her "things." The most basic equipment was unavailable: ". . .can't even find a paper clip." Absent from her workspace, she said she was "wasting time" even though she appeared to be quite busy. The frustration and discomfort elicited by this experience led her to make the strongest statement she ever made during the period of observation: "I hate this."

Her discomfort was related to concerns about her own efficiency. It was difficult, under the circumstances, to keep accurate track of new registrants. Some were registering at the school, some at the church where school was temporarily held during construction. Edna Brown was continually concerned about the "class list." For a while the original, which was the only current list, could not be found, and she spent a lot of anxious time looking for it. Losing control of the class list meant that her "count," the number of currently registered students, might be inaccurate. It also meant that she could not be certain at any given moment about the location of a particular child, because other staff would sometimes assign children to the classrooms.

She was also unable to keep track of "her" staff. Schedules were not available and there was no system of direct communication with teachers. Locating a teacher meant finding that person in the building. If the teacher was on a break or had left the building for any reason, his or her whereabouts were unknown to the secretary. Edna Brown faced several situations where she unsuccessfully attempted to locate someone. One day the custodian could not be found after a child vomited in the nurse's office. It was up to Edna to clean the mess. At "her" school, she said, she would have a wall chart where all schedules would be noted. Without this aid she was handicapped in performing her function of "knowing where people are."

The secretary's ownership of the office space was also evident in the decorations at Washington School where the walls displayed evidence of Diane Green's accomplishments.

At Grant School Elsie Lavender kept a canister with writing equipment and a small stack of recycled paper on her desk "for the teachers to use," she said. It was clear that, although she was sharing the space, it was *her* space. The same secretary became very upset when she found the electric pencil sharpener broken. Someone had apparently continued to use it after it was full of shavings causing the motor to get burned out. Her anger, she explained, was at "their laziness." She retaliated by putting the broken sharpener in the teachers' workroom and bringing the unbroken one from there to the office.

The secretaries seldom leave the office. The location of the office, its physical arrangement, and the resources available there are an integral part of the secretaries' activities. Differences in office layouts contribute to differences in opportunities for the secretaries to interact with the staff.

The presence of a teachers' area nearby, as at Washington School, provided the setting for a continuous flow of teachers through the office. Such traffic contributed to congestion in the office but also gave rise to many informal exchanges.

The mailboxes are another center of attraction in school offices. At Fillmore the teachers' lounge was distant from the secretary's desk, but the mailboxes were nearby and served to attract teachers to the secretary's vicinity. The same was true at Alvarez School. At Grant School, where the teachers' lounge and the mailboxes were away from the secretary's workspace, the photocopier created a similar possibility for interactions. There was a constant flow of teachers and staff in the neighborhood of the copier. As they waited their turn, they might engage the secretary in conversations that often provided opportunities for work-related exchanges. They also provided opportunities for district "gossip" and requests for the secretary's help.

Copiers are not only benevolent centers for professional interaction, they are also a source of noise and of mechanical problems that the secretaries are called upon to fix.

At most schools in the study this task was implicitly assigned to the school secretary. At Alvarez School it was an explicit assignment—part of the division of responsibility agreed on by the staff as a whole, but not to Mary's liking. "I really don't enjoy that sort of thing, and the Xerox machine is quite a ways from my office and there are days when it does not like me at all . . . so I find myself some days barely able to make another trip in there . . . usually when you're trying to get something done and you can't."

Implicit or explicit, the care and feeding of photocopiers is an important part of the secretary's work in all the schools. The amount of time spent in this task depends on the quality of the particular copier. During one two-hour observation at Grant School, Elsie spent the whole period trying to get the copier to work.

In summary, the school office is the secretary's base of operations. It is also the physical and operational center of the school. Although the secretaries seldom leave the office, teachers are continually passing through the area during their breaks and before and after school. At those times they take the opportunity to check their mailboxes or use the photocopying machine. These locations in the vicinity of the school secretary provide opportunities for the teachers to interact with the secretary about all sorts of school and personal matters.

The School Day

The level of activity in the school offices varies with the rhythm of the school. The secretary is usually the first one (except for the custodian) to arrive at the school, often in search of some quiet work time before the official opening of the school day. The teachers' arrival signals the beginning of the day's activities that continue, in crescendo, until the students' arrival, and diminishes abruptly with the school bell. Mornings are usually slower until the beginning of the lunch periods, which are marked by a constant flow of teachers through the office. Activity levels off during the early afternoon and increases again at dismissal when it reaches its daily maximum as students, teachers, and even parents bring their problems to the secretary. She usually remains at the school long after everyone else has departed. This is the time to catch up.

People in the School Office

One principal said, "As the office manager, school secretaries have a responsibility to fill in and be all things to all people." This statement is particularly true in offices where the secretary is the only adult available. Where other adults are present, she may be able to share the responsibility.

According to the elementary school secretaries' responses to the survey, most of them are alone in their offices. Only about one third of those responding have part-time clerical assistance. School nurses and counselors often occupy nearby offices, but this is also part-time work (sometimes no more than one day a week). About 5% of the secretaries responding work in schools that share their principal with another school. This is lower than the national figure.

The 1988 study of elementary and middle school (K-8) principals conducted by the National Association of Elementary School Principals (NAESP) reports that 12% of the principals surveyed served more than one school. My data suggests that dual responsibilities are most likely to occur with smaller schools; however, several of the sharing schools had as many as 200 students and at least one had 500. This means that in many schools, including some rather large ones, the school secretary is the only person in the office for at least half the time. On the other hand, about one fourth of the secretaries reported having a vice-principal at the school.

The complexity of the school may also be expected to contribute to the activities in the school office. In the survey, I used the number of special programs housed in the school, as well as the number of extracurricular activities, as indicators of school complexity.

More than two thirds of the secretaries responding to the survey reported there were between three and four special programs (such as bilingual or special education) as well as from two to four extracurricular activities in their schools. In addition, about three quarters of the secretaries reported the existence of active parent-teacher organizations and volunteer programs in their schools.

At the six case-study schools, the number of people in the office varied according to their district's policies. The four schools in District 1 had been recently assigned full-time attendance clerks in an effort to facilitate school-community relations. All of the clerks lived within the school's attendance area and most had children attending the school. They were mainly responsible for keeping track of absent children and contacting their parents. This service was particularly helpful at schools with large numbers of children who were speakers of other languages. All but one of these attendance aides were fluent in Spanish, the home language of many of the students. The two secretaries in District 2 schools had no clerical assistance in their offices.

The presence of clerical aides relieved the secretaries of some telephone duties and allowed them the luxury of being absent. Neither district provided substitutes for the secretaries for absences of less than 3 days. This meant that, upon her return, the secretary would encounter a deskful of delayed work. This, and the guilt of not being available when needed, discouraged the secretaries' absences. The newly appointed clerks in District 1 did not have much schooling or experience. Therefore they could not do much of the secretary's work, but they could satisfy the need for that ever-present body in the office.

There were part-time nurses at all six case-study school offices and four schools also had part-time counselors. Secretaries often relied on these counselors as surrogates to the principal during the latter's absence. None of the six schools shared their principal and none had been assigned vice-principals.

In terms of school complexity, the schools observed exhibited characteristics similar to those of the secretaries who responded to the survey. All six schools housed at least four special programs, as well as several extracurricular activities. All had active parent-teacher organizations, some of which relied heavily on the secretary's help, and most also had volunteer programs. In two schools the secretaries ran a babysitting network that allowed parents in need of care for their children to connect with parents offering such services. This activity, as well as many others observed, was not considered an extra, but was part and parcel of the school secretary's day.

The abundance of activities beyond the expected classroom organization suggests the complexity of the school office. Each additional program entails separate lists of participants, record forms to be filled, schedules to be kept, reports to be completed, and maintenance of contracts with either the school district or community members. All of these activities are usually entrusted to the school secretary, and they bring her in contact with a varied clientele.

THE SECRETARY'S CLIENTELE

Schools differ from other public institutions in that the clients are compelled to accept their services. Although choice among hospitals or among social agencies is possible, school attendance, usually at a prescribed site, is compulsory. This is an essential characteristic of the school-community relationship (Lortie, 1977), and one that has important implications for the principal and, by extension, the school secretary. If conflict and alienation are to be minimized, the institution must respond to the interests of the clients (Iannaccone, 1978). This responsibility is formally assigned to the principal (Morris, Crowson, Hurwitz, & Porter-Gehrie, 1981), but the daily interactions, the flow of visitors, and the telephone also provide a multitude of informal opportunities for communication that fall upon the school secretary. This is especially true during the 11% of the time that principals are away from their offices (Morris et al., 1981) when the secretary may assume actual, if not official, control of the building. Thus the school secretary may play a critical role in the development of positive or negative school-community relationships.

As was noted by Vinnicombe (1983), the work of the secretary varies according to the context in which it is performed. An earlier section cited comments by two secretaries pointing out differences they had experienced when they moved from the business to the school setting. They remarked on the unpredictability of activities in the school office and contrasted it to the established routines of the business setting. Part of that unpredictability is related to the varied clientele served by the school.

As a public setting, the school differs from a business office in the breadth of its clientele. The school secretary is not only responsible to members of the internal community. In the schools all tax-paying citizens are entitled to have their say; everyone has a stake in what happens there. The school secretary, therefore, has many clients: the children who are directly affected by the school program, their parents, the teachers, the support staff, and the principal; and beyond the school building, the school district officials and the community.

Variety of Clients

The school secretary's world is filled with human interactions. The secretaries observed were involved in anywhere from 15 to 40 or more interactions during a 2 hour period, not including phone calls. Many of those interactions were brief and cursory; others required great expenditure of effort. Sometimes it was the intellectual effort needed to straighten out a problem. At other times it was the effort required to maintain composure in a difficult situation.

Most of the secretary-client interactions observed were with members of the school community including all the people who worked in the school plus the students, their parents, and regular volunteers. Some secretaries had close relationships with certain teachers or aides or with the principal, but all tended to have a special relationship to the collective school community. This relationship was expressed through their use of the possessive: "my teachers," "my parents," "my students." One day Sandy Pink excitedly welcomed me with the news that "one of my students," from her former school, was being transferred to Hayes School. Her statement reflected the special relationship between the school secretary and the schoolchildren.

Students

When asked to whom, among their many clients, they owed their primary responsibility, five of the six case-study secretaries unequivocally responded that it was to the children. This responsibility was best expressed by Mary Lime who believed that people outside of the school setting trusted the school secretary as the "keeper of their children." The strength of the secretaries' relationship with the students was also evident in their responses to two questions in the survey. The first one asked the secretaries to rank their various clients in order of preference. The second asked them to rank the same clients "according to the priorities you are likely to assign them." Their answers were interesting and suggest a conflict faced by the school secretary.

In response to the question about their work preferences, secretaries ranked working with students highest among the choices offered. It was closely followed by secretarial tasks. These two choices were ranked number one more often than any of the other seven choices, which included working with administrators, teachers, parents, and community. The latter two received the lowest ranks among the seven categories offered.

Secretaries' responses to the second question, which asked them to rank, in order of priority, administrators, teachers, parents, students, district personnel, and school secretaries in other buildings, elicited a slightly different response. In this case, administrators were ranked highest, students were next, and teachers were third. The majority of the respondents gave the first rank to either administrators or students while "other school secretaries" were assigned the lowest rank.

Responses to these two questions suggest that, although these secretaries may personally prefer to work with the students, their job responsibilities demand they give a higher priority to the school administrators. This inference is supported by the high priority the responding secretaries attached to "working with children" as a reason for their career choice.

Teachers

Executive secretaries in the business world are responsible to one boss. For school secretaries the boss is the school principal, but the range of their responsibilities extends far beyond that individual. As Mary Lime explained, "You keep track of so many different things, supplies, machinery, and doing for the children, that you really have a lot of interaction with the teachers and staff."

The secretaries' relationships with the teachers were full of ambivalence. On the one hand, the secretaries tended to speak highly of the teachers in their schools. On the other, they were often frustrated because the teachers would fail to follow directions or to get things accurately completed and to the office on time. Edna Brown spoke of "my teachers" as "just a true delight to work with . . . a caring bunch . . . ." But she also said, "A lot of times I get irritated . . . . A lot of them will come and barge in and say, '[Edna] I need this . . . will you do this?' . . . and have no respect really for what I'm working on."

Elsie Lavender often spoke of being there to assist teachers and of the lack of recognition given teachers by the public. Her model for the school secretary was the woman who had held the job at her children's school where she had volunteered before assuming the secretarial position. That experienced secretary had taught her a number of ways in which a teacher's life could be made easier by the school secretary. Providing pens and pencils and note paper on her desk for the teachers to use is an example. However, Elsie also spoke of sending out memos in "language the teachers would understand" or of taking over part of the attendance calculations because the teachers did not "add the figures right."

At two of the schools, Alvarez and Washington, the relationship between the teachers and the secretary was closer to a "mutual admiration society." They spoke highly of each other often and consistently. "The secretary—she's the lifeline!" was proclaimed spontaneously by a first-year teacher at one of these schools when she learned about the study. And around Diane Green's desk at

Washington School, numerous certificates and pictures bore witness to the faculty's gratitude.

Parents

The secretaries could also become attached to some parents. Mary Lime held back tears one day when she told me that one of "my parents" had died suddenly. Two of the women's grandchildren and one daughter attended Alvarez School, and she had been a frequent visitor.

Alvarez School was also blessed with a large and helpful corps of volunteer parents. Mary noted how these parents called her during the summer to offer their help in the preparations for the opening of the school. I observed these eager helpers numerous times as they provided clerical assistance to the teachers and the secretary.

Sandy Pink at Hayes School and Kathy Orange at Fillmore also worked closely with their very active parent groups, particularly in the school's fund-raising activities. Kathy Orange was especially efficient in recruiting volunteers among parents whom she knew as neighbors in the area.

Parents could also be a source of concern as when Kathy Orange disapproved of a parent's willingness to bring her child's forgotten homework to the school; or when Sandy Pink was pressured by an influential parent who wanted her to change her child's classroom assignment.

For Elsie Lavender, parent complaints were one of the negative characteristics of her job. She explained that parents did not seem to understand that most people in the school were there "because we're concerned with what happens to the kids" and not just to get a paycheck. But in spite of those problems she believed that 95% of her interactions with parents were positive and that was what she tried to concentrate on.

My own observations also suggest that angry parents comprised only a tiny minority of the clients seen at the schools, and yet the "irate parent" was very much a part of each school's folklore. Most secretaries could describe a situation where they had been threatened verbally, and certain parents were said to play this role consistently.

At Dewey School everyone knew a certain parent as an "irate parent." This was the school that was temporarily housed at the church building while renovations were being completed at the school building. One day the daily kindergarten bus that transported children between the church and the school left one child behind. Everyone groaned—it had to be Mrs. Sanchez' son among all the children! True to form, a furious Mrs. Sanchez arrived at the church and confronted the first person she met—the school secretary. A very diplomatic Edna Brown soon placated her, apologized for the mistake, and resolved the problem.

This is not unique to any one school. For example, at Grant School a woman went abruptly through the office, right by the secretary, and into the principal's office. It was apparent that Elsie Lavender had chosen to ignore her. When asked, she said the woman had previously visited the campus and displayed enormous anger about the way her child had been disciplined. The principal had successfully calmed her down. Elsie was afraid to provoke her into another such outburst, so she let her go right through to his office.

Custodian

The secretary and the custodian are the major members of the school's classified staff. Their positions contrast with those of the teachers who are members of the professional staff. The secretary and the custodian might be expected, then, to have a special relationship based on this common bond. However, in the six case-study schools, the secretaries' relationship with the custodian was limited to a cursory professional relationship.

At one school the custodian's attempt to establish a closer relationship with the secretary was continually thwarted by her. He would come to the office with some information, and then sit and attempt to engage her in small talk. The secretary would deal with the situation and then turn her attention to her work.

At another school the custodian was rather gruff and sometimes difficult. The secretary gave him a lot of credit for his good work and tolerated his outbursts. But one day when both she and the principal were going to be away, she asked the principal to please hurry back to school after his meeting because a band from another school was coming to visit. She was afraid that the custodian would greet the visiting band in a rude manner.

Support staff and district personnel

The relationship between the secretaries and the support staff varied among the observed schools according to district and school-site guidelines. In most cases, the secretary was responsible for typing official reports issued by the various pupil-personnel staff such as the counselor or psychologist. Sometimes they also took care of some of the nurse's reports. This work could be time consuming and was often unexpected and rushed.

The secretaries were also unofficially charged with the task of orienting new personnel to the school's (and sometimes the district's) policies. During the first few days of her assignment to Fillmore School, the new nurse required a good portion of Kathy Orange's time. Kathy explained policies, connected the nurse with parents and showed her where to find what she needed.

The secretary's interactions with district personnel were mostly by telephone. Those secretaries (Sandy Pink, Diane Green and Edna Brown) who had worked in the district office had an advantage in that they could build on those established relationships. I did not meet many district level personnel during the course of my observations in the schools. As a result of the frequency of telephone interactions the secretaries had with some of them, however, I managed to learn the names of several district emloyees. Rose, in the transportation office, was one of those. In the schools with busing programs, hardly a day went by without a call to or from Rose.

Sometimes the secretaries expressed resentment of certain district personnel. In District 2 Mary Lime and Sandy Pink were unhappy with the new computers dedicated to the maintenance of attendance records. These machines, intended to reduce their work, had added to it instead. Absences had to be entered by using the students' nine-digit identification number rather than their names. The secretaries knew most students by name, but could not memorize the long numbers. Since the teachers recorded absences by name, the secretary had to look up each child's number in order to enter the absence and then again to correct the record if the child arrived later. The secretaries believed that, had they been consulted, the problem could have been avoided.

The amount of busy work demanded from the teachers by some school district personnel also concerned the secretaries. Elsie Lavender believed that the demands from one administrator verged on the abusive, so she collected all the memos and requests sent by that person to the school and displayed them for the principal. He was able to understand the problem, and thereafter sought ways to reduce it.

Conflicts

Given the number of clients, and their potential for conflict with one another, it is not surprising that secretaries sometimes find themselves in the middle of a conflict. When they were asked about such situations, most of the secretaries and principals interviewed were able to give specific examples.

For Edna Brown, "being in the middle" occurred often. She explained that during lunch, teachers aired their complaints and she listened. Later the principal might complain to her about the teachers. She said that she sometimes tried to mediate their problems without making specific references, but she was very careful. As she put it, "I won't lie to my boss, but I won't squeal to him either . . . ." Her principal, Mr. John, recognized the difficult position she was in, between himself and the teachers. She also got caught, he noted, between priorities he had set and demands made by particular teachers. In such cases he said he tried to support her because, "if I expect her to support me, I've got to support her."

Kathy Orange's principal spoke about her unusual position as a parent and a staff member. He knew there were times when, as a parent, she had not been happy with her child's instruction; but as a staff member, she remained loyal to the instructional program.

Elsie Lavender had no trouble recalling an incident when she was in the middle of a conflict during her eventful first year on the job. The principal had been away for a few days when Elsie registered a child and placed him, according to the numbers, in a classroom. A couple of days later the mother came to the school and "cursed me out royally." She "wanted the boy out of that classroom"; if he were not removed, she was intent on keeping him home. Elsie said she considered the alternatives and decided that the boy's attendance in school was more important than his classroom assignment, so she went ahead and made the change. She also warned the mother that the principal, Mr. Ulysses, would make a final decision upon his return. This action satisfied the mother but angered the teacher to whom the child had been originally assigned. She was furious at the secretary and accused her of not supporting the teachers.

By the time Mr. Ulysses returned, the child was doing much better in the new classroom, and he left him there. The teacher asked the teachers' association to intervene and Elsie had to participate in a hearing. After hearing both sides, the association representatives decided not to support the teacher.

Elsie said the experience had left her "a little bit squeamish," but she still believed she had done the right thing by keeping the boy in school. She concluded, "My primary objective is for the kids to have a good education."

The principal recalled the same incident as an example of how Elsie could get caught in the middle. He said his recollection about the details was fuzzy, but he remembered the conclusion. The teacher's action was apparently motivated, at least in part, by complaints she had against him. Elsie got caught in the middle because the teacher was trying to make a case that the principal was not doing his job.

Mr. Rutherford, principal at Hayes School, voiced his concern that the school secretary's many clients might take advantage of her kindness with too many demands. He argued that the secretary needed to be forceful in maintaining all relationships at an equal distance. This was especially important, he noted, during the principal's absence when the secretary might be placed in an awkward position by staff members who considered her "an easier hit." He said the principal needed to support the school secretary to ensure that everyone understood that her major responsibility was to be director of the school office.

Sandy Pink was quite aware of the problems of finding herself in the middle. She said she always found it hard to decide whether or not she should tell the principal certain things. She remembered a situation where a parent who was very active in the parent-teacher organization wanted to have her child placed in a certain classroom. She did not want to accept the placement recommended by the kindergarten teacher and the principal. The woman tried to use Sandy as a go-between with the principal. Finding herself caught in the middle, the secretary tried "to be positive" and encouraged the mother to follow the principal's advice. Despite Sandy's efforts, the woman persisted and eventually had her wish. As it turned out, the child did not do well in that classroom and had to be placed back in the one to which he had been originally assigned.

When asked if there were times when she had found herself in the middle, Mary Lime also responded affirmatively. She explained that parents unhappy about their child's school experience would complain to her. She said she tried to develop a "good, friendly attitude toward them. And if they're negative just to work extra hard." When they sought her out about a problem in the school, she said she tried to be positive about the faculty member who was involved. She noted that she might "feed them something good about that teacher" because, she added, "[teachers] might have one little thing that bugs the parents, but they have 99 other things that are really good." At times, Mary said, she had also recommended to dissatisfied staff members that they bring their concerns directly to the principal.

Ms. Alonso, principal at Alvarez School, did not think that teacher-secretary conflicts were likely to arise at Alvarez because Mary Lime was so highly respected by the staff. She said her decisions were respected because everyone knew they were generally carefully thought through.

In summary, many different clients compete daily for the attention of the school secretary. This situation creates demands on her time and emotional resources that are far in excess of those placed on secretaries in the business setting. Faced with varied and sometimes conflicting demands, school secretaries must learn to carefully navigate through them, particularly as they operate in a situation that grants them only intermittent power. It is a measurement of the quality of the women who hold these jobs that, for the most part, they are able to carry out this difficult task successfully.

QUALITY OF WORK

Judging by the responses of the six secretaries interviewed for this study, school secretaries are extremely satisfied with their jobs. For Edna Brown, the job offered stimulation: "I love being with people . . . doing a variety of things. It just keeps me stimulated." Sandy Pink effusively stated, "The last couple of years have probably been the happiest in my life . . . . I know my job has . . . a lot to do with it." And Kathy Orange, at Fillmore School, found pleasure in the work because "it does take thinking."

The enthusiasm of the interviewed secretaries was mirrored in their responses to the survey. Responding secretaries described their positions as interesting, enjoyable, and important. Although most of these women chose the job because of its compatibility with their children's schedule, they seem to have found the job quite satisfying. The vast majority said they would make the same choice again. They were less certain about recommending this job to their children, however. In their marginal comments they suggested that, in that question, they were forced to face economic realities. Slightly more than half decided they could not recommend this position to their children. This reaction provides an interesting parallel between school secretaries and teachers who tend to be enthusiastic about their jobs but hesitant in recommending it to their children.

The secretaries' most honest expression of satisfaction with their work was perhaps most evident in their responses to the two open-ended questions of the survey. The first one asked: What are you most proud of in your work? And the last question asked them for any additional comments.

Pride and the Secretaries' Work

Ability to help others

Almost all of the elementary school secretaries who participated in the survey associated their feelings of pride in their jobs with either personal satisfaction or with satisfaction in the accomplishment of tasks. The secretaries expressed pride in their ability to help principals, children, and teachers (listed here in order of frequency of mention), once again reflecting the breadth of the clientele they serve:

> "Help that I can provide staff and students, parents and community"
> "The satisfaction that I may have helped some small child along his or her way"

In a few cases, specific help to teachers, principals, and/or parents was singled out for emphasis:

> "I am always ready to help teachers."
> "I feel that my hard work as a school secretary helped my principal to be chosen as the outstanding principal of [this] district last year."
> "I feel that I am able to help parents and students who have problems."

Contributions to the educational process

The secretaries' pride in their ability to help was associated with their responsibilities as contributors to the educational process. They commented on their role in establishing the proper atmosphere in the school office and in providing the help necessary to support instruction.

> "I am in a position to help the public schools operate efficiently and benefit students by example of [*sic*] giving them pride in themselves by showing interest."
> "I help to create a warm and friendly atmosphere in our school as well as the office."
> "Accurate records, helping students and teachers—just to see one student accomplish something he thought he could not do makes me feel so good."

The responding secretaries also expressed pride in their direct contribution to the educational endeavor and often identified themselves with the teaching staff. They associated the efficient operation of the school with the effective delivery of instruction.

> "My contribution to the molding of young people's ideas and feelings about themselves and my contribution to the team effort, with teachers and administrators, that accomplishes this"

"To manage our office efficiently, to support the principal and teachers,
   to provide the best possible education to our children"
"That I can be a living example to young children"
"I can't be a teacher, but I can do my part to help education."

The secretaries often expressed pride in the special relationships
they have with children, teachers, principals, and sometimes parents.

"Love of children; friendship of teachers; appreciation of principal"
"My rapport with teachers, parents, students, and administrators"
"Being loved and remembered by parents"

Competence and efficiency

Pride was also associated with feelings of competence and efficiency expressed as being organized and having a "smoothly running school." Respondents expressed pride in a job well done
and/or specific tasks they had accomplished, such as modernizing
certain procedures.

"The opportunity to feel that I have made a vital and necessary contri-
   bution to the efficient and smooth running of our local school"
"Efficiency. Ability to call each child and parent by name"
"The smooth operation of the school, getting the tasks done"
"Keeping the office organized and running smoothly, accurate book-
   keeping"

In order to ensure an accurate representation of the elementary
school secretaries' perceptions, the last question in the survey
asked respondents to add any additional comments about their
work or about the survey itself. The majority of the sample
answered this request, and many did so in lengthy, sometimes
detailed, multipage statements. Their responses clustered around
three categories: relationships, rewards, and love.

Relationships, Rewards, and Love

Relationships

The majority of their comments about relationships were positive and related to principals. Negative comments were associated

sometimes with teachers and principals, but always with the district administration; that is, mention of district administrators was always made in tandem with a negative comment and usually related to status concerns. For example:

"Our school district administrators (not the principal, those at the administration building) still treat us as second-class citizens."
"We elementary secretaries are very dedicated, competent and work very hard; our higher administrators and board of education don't realize this."
"We would like to change central office attitude about 'the girls in the front office.' "

Negative comments about teachers were often related to status differences; for example:

"Some teachers feel the secretary is a 'personal handmaiden.' "
"Least enjoyable is teachers' attitude toward clerical personnel,—condescending, unappreciative, and superior in general."

Given this open-ended, anonymous opportunity to comment about their jobs, it is surprising that negative comments about teachers by secretaries were not common. Positive comments were far more frequent.

"My overtime is given, not asked for, as I feel the need to be available before and after classes for the teachers."
"I do little extras for my teachers. They appreciate it, and I am treated as an equal, both professionally and socially."

Comments made by these secretaries about their principals were mostly positive as well. Most referred to the good working relationship they had with their bosses, although several were critical of their principals. These criticisms were usually associated with the principal's lack of efficiency and/or leadership:

"I'm fortunate to be a secretary to a principal who's excellent in administration, is open to suggestions, and gives me free rein as long as I do my job well and completely."
"I've worked for three principals and have enjoyed each one and admired them for their individual personalities and ways of administering the school."

"Administrators I've had in the past are more efficient and effective than the one I have now. An inefficient administrator makes a dull school with low morale."

"I enjoy my job thoroughly, but it has been extremely frustrating,—this is due to the lack of a leader. The principal is a young man who was a former teacher. He took administration courses but lacks know-how dealing with staff and general management."

Rewards

Most of the negative feelings of these elementary school secretaries were associated with the dearth of rewards such as salary and recognition. The secretaries made strong and frequent statements about their low salaries and about the lack of recognition and appreciation bestowed on them. They tended to blame school district administrators rather than their principals for these problems. Sometimes their negative comments about salary and recognition were tempered with positive comments reflecting their enjoyment of the job. In other cases their complaints were associated with comments about the disproportionate amount of responsibility placed on elementary school secretaries.

"The elementary school secretary is one of [the] most underpaid for the amount of work done."

"I love the job, but we don't get recognition given the responsibilities we have to assume."

"I love my job and would enjoy going to work every day except that I receive more and more responsibility without compensation or recognition. Speaking to anyone above the principal falls on deaf ears, so I hesitate to discuss my feelings with the principal as I feel I'm putting her in the middle."

"The secretary is given little recognition or appreciation. Recently two positions opened in the district, one requesting a principal's secretary, the other a cleaner. The latter's starting salary was $1,000 more per year . . . . There's great inequity here."

Love

The third and last category under which the responses to the request for additional comments were clustered was love. Most of these were associated with the job: "I love my job and have nothing asked of me I don't enjoy doing," or "I just have to say I love my job."

One secretary expressed the opinion of many in her positive reaction to the survey: "I loved filling out this survey! We elementary school secretaries need all the help we can get. Thank you."

The school secretaries observed, interviewed, and surveyed for this study appeared to be very satisfied with their jobs. Although the salary is low and recognition beyond the walls of the school nonexistent, these women were consistently positive in their appraisals of their jobs and optimistic about their contribution.

The secretaries responding to the survey expressed a strong commitment to education and to their role as contributors to the educational endeavor. They made a direct link between the pedestrian office routines they perform and the provision of a good educational environment. This connection is similar to that made by Rutter et al. (1979) and by Barr, Dreeben, and Wiratachi (1983) and discussed in Chapter 2. The educational role assumed by these respondents differs significantly from the secretary's role described in the official job descriptions and discussed in the following section. Those descriptions emphasize the technical aspects of the job and give little indication of a connection between the secretary's work and the school's effectiveness.

The secretaries, it seems, derive their pride from their helping role and in so doing they ally themselves with the many members of the helping professions: social workers, nurses, and geriatric caregivers who, like them, are mostly lower-paid women.

JANE OF ALL TRADES

In this section the secretary's multiple roles in the elementary school are reviewed. What the official job descriptions have to say about the school secretary's job is reported first, and then these official expectations are compared to the descriptions of the job offered by the secretaries and their principals, and the execution of the job as I observed it. The impact that specific characteristics of the school have on the secretary's work load is then discussed, followed by a description of some activities regularly carried out by the school secretary. The section ends with a discussion of the secretaries' opinions about activities they do not think should be assigned to them.

The multiplicity of roles fulfilled by the school secretary was well summarized by one of the principals interviewed. When asked about tasks such as first aid that the school secretary was often required to assume beyond the usual secretarial duties, Principal Ulysses said, "She's got to handle them . . . . There's no other way to take care of them." For this reason, he said, the secretary's job ends up being, "a multiple kind of position—parent, nurse, friend, psychologist—but that's part of the job." This description of the secretary's job offered by one of the interviewed principals was borne out by many observations but was not reflected in the official job descriptions.

What the Job Descriptions Say

Twenty-seven job descriptions were sent in by secretaries responding to the survey. Each of the representative documents included a section listing the responsibilities of elementary school secretaries, which tended to be the longest section in the document. After aggregating the lists from the different documents, I found extreme diversity in the school districts' expectations of their building secretaries.

A simple count of all unduplicated responsibilities listed in this set of job descriptions added up to 83 different tasks, which were divided into nine categories as follows:

1. Tasks related to the principal's work
2. Tasks related to the maintenance of records
3. Tasks related to the school finances
4. Tasks related to student support
5. Tasks related to the support of the instructional staff
6. Tasks related to the securing and distribution of materials
7. Standard secretarial tasks
8. Public relations tasks
9. Odd tasks that did not easily fit into one of the above categories

The number of individual tasks included within each of the main (1-8) categories varied between 7 and 16. The largest group of individual tasks (16) fell within the standard secretarial tasks category. The next largest group (11) clustered under tasks related to the maintenance of records. The smallest group of tasks was devoted to the securing and distribution of supplies and materials.

The set of unclassifiable tasks included only three: cover for nurse, voter registrar, and coordination of fund-raising drives.

My analysis of the responsibilities assigned to the secretary in these job descriptions indicates that the districts place their emphasis on the standard secretarial tasks. Typing, filing, and composing letters all fall within this category. The emphasis in this section is consistent with the emphasis found in the summary statements and qualifications sections. In all three sections—summary statement, qualifications statement, and responsibilities statement—the tasks most frequently mentioned are those related to the traditional secretarial position. The skills listed as necessary to qualify for the position are notably similar.

An interesting characteristic of this array of responsibilities is their reach across different settings. If one conceives of school systems as sets of concentric circles with the principal at the center and expanding circles representing teachers, students, the district, and the community, then the tasks assigned to the school secretary in these job descriptions cut right across all of these circles. They begin in the center with support of the principal and stretch all the way to the edge with "establishing and maintaining a good relationship with other offices, schools, and government agencies" (See Figure 3.1).

These descriptions had another noticeable characteristic. The tasks school secretaries were expected to perform provided examples of all the different types of clerical work described by Lopata (1984). She divided clerical jobs into four categories to indicate the diversity of positions available under the general rubric of "clerical": clerks, receptionists, secretaries, and high-complexity office support workers or executive secretaries. Lopata described each of these categories as follows:

Clerks—relatively unskilled individuals who are assigned the mindless daily routines required in an office

Receptionists—concentrate on the social relations aspect

Secretaries—perform the standard functions for an entire office

Executive secretaries or assistants to. . .—have more authority and fexibility

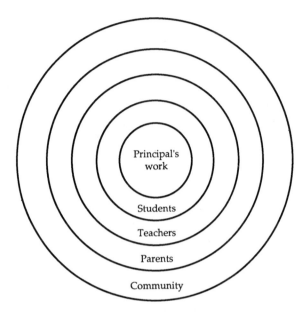

Figure 3.1 The Reach of School Secretary's Responsibilities

As described through the responsibilities listed in these documents, the elementary school secretary is charged with carrying
out tasks that are representative of all four categories, from simple
filing and recordkeeping to assisting the executive, i.e., the principal.

What Secretaries Said in the Survey

Responses to survey questions about their responsibilities
revealed a great deal of variation among the secretaries. This
variety makes it difficult to define the elementary school secretaries' job with precision since the assignment of tasks appears to
be heavily dependent on the specific school and principal. It is
possible to see, however, that a few tasks are consistently within
the secretary's purview though others may sometimes be assigned
to clerks or may be performed by the principal.

It was clear, for example, that school secretaries are the recordkeepers; 96% of the respondents said they were responsible for those tasks. The telephone is also solidly within the secretary's sphere of responsibility; 94% said they take care of it and the remaining 6% do so "sometimes." Similarly, school correspondence is almost always handled by the secretary. The staff bulletin, the administrator's paperwork, supplies, and the parent's newsletter were also reported to be usually assigned to the school secretary. But surprisingly, first aid was rated higher than any of these tasks. Results showed that 98% of the respondents have either full (most likely) or partial responsibility for this task (see Table 3.1).

According to the responses to the survey, typing for the teachers is not commonly done by the school secretary. Although it is reportedly the least likely of 19 tasks to be performed by the school secretaries, 25% of them are still routinely responsible for teacher typing. Someone else, perhaps the principal or vice-principal, takes care of securing substitutes. But a few secretaries commented that this task was indeed one of theirs, and since it was usually handled before and after school hours, it was unpaid. Responsibility for the school budget and, to a lesser extent, for registers and attendance, is apparently also often shared.

The breadth of responsibilities assigned to the elementary school secretary does not seem to faze the holders of these positions. Even as anonymous respondents to the survey, their spontaneous written comments along the margins repeatedly expressed pleasure in this characteristic of their jobs: "I find the variety most enjoyable."

What the Secretaries Were Observed Doing

Observations conducted for this study confirmed both the variety of tasks performed by the secretaries and their enjoyment of this variety. I had originally planned to count the number and type of interactions in which the secretaries engaged during the school day in order to report percentages of time spent in different activities. This proved to be impossible. Saxe (1968) reports that in a 1961 analysis of clerical duties in Chicago schools, secretaries had found

Table 3.1 Percent of Sample Reporting Responsibility for Selected Tasks

Tasks	Yes	Only Sometimes
Recordkeeping	96	2
Telephones	94	6
Requisitions	91	7
Correspondence	90	9
First Aid	81	17
Classified Payroll	78	3
Administrator's Paperwork	75	20
Student Permanent Records	75	17
Supplies	75	17
Slush Fund	75	6
Parent Newsletter	73	15
Attendance	72	21
Registers	67	10
Teacher Payroll	63	3
School Budget	53	19
Administrator's Calendar	50	30
Securing Substitutes	45	39
Teacher Typing	25	60

such careful tabulation impossible as well. They blamed the difficulty on the many variables and constant interruptions encountered through the day. The popular image of the secretary as an octopus-like being attests to the general impression the public has of her role (See Figure 3.1).

Figure 3.2 A Popular View of a School Secretary
Source: Reprinted from *Learning* magazine, School secretary promotion, 1985. Springhouse
Corporation, Springhouse, PA 19477.

Variety

The reality as observed is not far from that popular impression.
School secretaries often attend to several things at once and the
specific tasks are also totally unpredictable.

At Hayes School, a small school with an enrollment of 244, seven
children enrolled on one day in January, almost 3% of the school's
total enrollment. At Washington School on the first day of classes,
a kindergarten boy fell and broke his arm. The secretary was the
first one at his side and the one who called his home and made the
necessary arrangements for his care while reassuring the scared
little boy.

There was no nurse during one day at Fillmore School when a
"severe and profound" special education student had to be "med-
icated." The student was an overweight 20-year-old woman. The
secretary described the scene: "Well, this morning I got kicked in
the rear . . . had to go down and give T., in severe and profound
[mental impairment], her medicine. Well, she's a real big girl, very

strong, so we had to prop her with a bean bag . . . . She doesn't like her medicine so B. is trying to sit on her hands . . . so I can just do it . . . . Well, we finally got that one but . . . she wouldn't . . . swallow it so . . . I'm blowing on her face to make her swallow the medicine. Then we had to give her the second, two of them, two teaspoons . . . .I have never seen T. like that."

At Dewey School a classroom was left without a teacher, and someone had to take care of it. The secretary was the only adult available, so she assumed the responsibility. In each of these instances the secretary was the "wild card" who picked up the required role.

Although clerical work—including record-keeping, filling out forms, typing, and maintaining files—took a good portion of the secretary's time at the sites observed, there was no predicting how a given day might go. Some days the secretary would spend all day sitting at the typewriter, perhaps working on the reports for state awards. Another day she might be so busy with other things that she would never sit at all. One morning at Hayes School the secretary arrived at 7:50. She did not sit down until 8:30 a.m. There were many such occasions.

Simultaneity

The secretaries' activities were also characterized by simultaneity. These women were adept at engaging in several tasks at the same time. One day Kathy Orange received a telephone call from a mother offering her help to a teacher who was taking students on a field trip that day. Kathy put the call on hold while she called the teacher on the intercom. She was speaking to the teacher when the principal walked by and suggested that Kathy call a certain sixth-grade boy to check if he was the owner of a jacket found in the playground. The cafeteria supervisor, who happened to be standing nearby, overheard the conversation about the field trip and asked the secretary whether it would affect the lunch schedule. In about one minute Kathy Orange interacted with four different people. She received an affirmative response from the teacher about the mother's offer to help. She relayed this response to the mother. She told the cafeteria supervisor that the field trip would not affect her lunch schedule, and she heard and retained the principal's request regarding calling the boy about the jacket. She proceeded to fulfill that request as soon as she hung up the telephone. The simultaneity evident in this example was typical of the behavior of the school secretaries observed.

Some secretaries seemed to derive their energy from the agitation in the school office. For example, after the telephones stopped ringing at the end of a very busy day, after dealing with eight different cases of missed buses or stops, Kathy Orange commented: "[I] don't know if I can handle it, it's so quiet . . . reorganizing my mind . . . get it going again."

Contributors to the Secretary's Work Load

Two conditions appeared to have the most effect on the pace and variety of the secretary's workday: the student population served by the school, and the availability of a nurse at the school.

At Fillmore School, where 65% of the students were bused in, a large amount of the school secretary's time was spent on busing problems. Most new entrants required arrangements for transportation. The bulk of these were the responsibility of the district office that made assignments according to the bus routes. But with the school's 45% mobility ratio, almost half the student body changed throughout the year. Most of these changes were reflected in the busing arrangements, and the school secretary attended to them. In addition, changes taking place in the families, such as separations and changes in employment, often required adjustments in transportation. Beyond these arrangements there were the daily misses of children who failed to get on the bus, or got into the wrong bus or off at the wrong stop. These misses made the school's arrival and departure periods very busy ones for the secretary.

The presence or absence of a nurse also affected the secretary greatly. One secretary spent three fourths of a two-hour observation period attending to sick children or speaking to their parents. None of the schools in this study had more than part-time nursing service assigned to them. In some schools a registered nurse (RN) and a health aide came on alternate days. In other schools the RN came in for a few hours daily. Unfortunately, children's discomforts and emergencies cannot be easily synchronized with the nurse's schedule. Even when part-time assistance was available, there were days when the nurse (or aide) was absent or when the position was vacant.

Vacancies affected all four of the schools in District 1 at one time or another during the period of observation. At one school there was no nurse for several weeks. Since two or three schools shared the position, interviews conducted in order to hire a replacement were cumbersome, requiring many participants. In one case the person hired lasted only a few weeks and then resigned because, according to the secretary, "she was too good" and the pay, she added, "too low to keep her in a very demanding job." During the intervening period it was, of course, up to the school secretary to handle the job.

On the other hand, the presence or absence of the principal tended to make little difference on the secretary's time. In most cases the principal's absence was not apparent to the observer unless the secretary alluded to it herself during a conversation. More messages might accumulate and some decisions might be postponed, but in general work went on as usual. Even staff bulletins were issued on schedule. At Grant School the principal was away for several days at a state meeting. He had written the bulk of the bulletin before leaving. The secretary filled in last-minute schedules and information and issued it as usual.

The lack of impact of the principal's absence on the secretary was also noted in the survey responses. The vast majority reported that the principal's absence did not make much difference in their work. Several did explain in unsolicited marginal comments that absences of one or two days had little effect, but prolonged absences affected the school a great deal. Others emphasized that while the principal's absence did have some effect, the school continued to run smoothly because "everyone assumes their responsibility."

Among the many roles performed by the school secretary, a few stood out as particularly important.

Public relations. A role in the school in public relations is commonly associated with the school secretary, and this notion was borne out by the observations. It was the secretary who was almost always encountered first by anyone coming to or calling the school. This was true even in those schools that had been assigned a clerical aide. The secretaries that were observed were all very conscious of their public relations role. The appearance of a visitor in the office elicited an invariably courteous and pleasant response. There was often a visible change in a secretary concentrating on her typing who was suddenly faced with a visitor. A smile and cheerful, "May I help you?" were quickly substituted for the frown of concentration.

Parents coming to enroll new students were usually regaled with explanations about school activities. At Hayes School they had a system where new enrollees were given all pertinent forms the first day, but children did not start until the next day. The secretary carefully explained this process and its reason, to each parent, saying, "That way the teacher can be ready for him tomorrow. She will have a desk and books all ready then." The explanation was clearly couched in terms of "this is the way *we* do it at Hayes," with emphasis on the advantages to be derived from this system. I did not observe any parents who reacted to this action negatively, even though it was usually obvious from the student's clothing and the brown bag carried, that the parent had expected the child to start school immediately.

Secretaries also had to respond to media requests. Although the final say was the principal's, they usually made all preliminary arrangements. It is likely that these initial interactions contributed to whatever impression of the school the media representatives carried back with them.

Kathy Orange dealt with such a request and became rather frustrated with the situation. The local television station wanted to do a story on the artist-in-residence program, but she knew that the time and day they had chosen would be inopportune. She tried, albeit unsuccessfully, to get them to change their plans so there would be minimal disruption to the classes. She explained that some of the students they wanted to videotape would not be available and that the principal would be at an out-of-town meeting at the time. Throughout the discussion the secretary explained all the different current and previous programs in the school and upcoming activities that might interest the media. She remained friendly and calm while she continued to advocate for a schedule better attuned to the school's schedule. When the principal

returned to the office he was also upset about the choice of date
and time. He tried, but was no more successful than she had been
in effecting a change.

Financial Tasks

The school secretaries' responsibility for maintaining financial
records is not obvious to the casual onlooker. After noticing the
frequency of monetary transactions in the schools, I decided to
include a question about this in the survey. The secretaries were
asked if they handled money in their job and if so, how much per
year on the average. Ninety-eight percent of the respondents
reported handling money, from $50 per year at one school to $1
million at another, with the average around $9,800 per year.

Sources of money varied across schools. Responses to the survey
indicate that in most cases combinations of several activities contributed to the school fund. Examples might be student activities,
sales, and faculty activities. Lunch money, including collecting,
extending credit, and bookkeeping were mentioned many times.
Book rentals, bookstore, and lost book fees were also mentioned,
as were building-use rental, book club orders, field trips, summer
and preschool tuition, and United Way contributions.

Also noted to be consistently in the hands of the secretary was
the school's "slush fund"—those small aggregations of money
collected through various fund-raising activities at the school such
as yearly photographs, candy sales, and bake sales. These accounts
allow the school administrator quick access to small amounts of
money for unexpected expenses, such as bus fare to allow a group
of students to attend a special exhibit, or money to buy materials
to make costumes for a play. Seventy-five percent of the secretaries
responding said they took care of these funds.

Rimer (1984) also noted the secretary's function as a collector and
recorder of money in the school. Teachers, he found, often regard
the secretary as the school's banker because she supplies change,
accepts checks, and computes balances of accounts.

The secretary is also often the keeper of the school budget. She
is the one most likely to know how much money has been spent in
a given category. Kathy Orange was wrestling with the budget one

day and explained that she did not know what to do. They were running out of money (this was early November) and Mr. Millard continued to approve requisitions. "I keep telling him there's no money, but it doesn't make any difference." She added that the problem was that teachers were supposed to turn in their requisitions by the previous summer but had failed to do so and now they kept coming up with requests. She believed that this situation was "their problem; they must not really want it."

Instruction

Although the conventional wisdom of school people assigns many roles to the school secretary, an instructional role is not usually among them. I was surprised to notice that some of the secretaries played an instructional role in their schools.

At Washington School, Diane Green played an important part in a major schoolwide activity. At this school a theme is selected each year and developed through daily morning messages, visual displays, and supplementary activities. During the year of the study the theme was "The 50 United States." Diane took care of the displays, including the large, wall-sized map in the office and large cut-outs of each state along the lunchroom walls. She identified the state of origin of each student and staff member and symbolized these with stars on each state. These records were kept up-to-date throughout the year. She also researched each of the states and prepared daily messages for the principal to announce during the opening activities each morning. In the principal's absence, Diane also listened to those students and teachers who were willing to take the "principal's challenge" and name all 50 states on the map. Among the six secretaries observed, Diane was most obviously active in instruction, but others also participated in instructional activities. They listened as children read to them; provided encouragement when students showed them their latest accomplishments; helped a child with schoolwork when such assistance was required, as Elsie Lavender was observed to do; or even took over a classroom, as Edna Brown did in an emergency.

A less obvious contribution of the secretaries to the instructional program was in minimizing interruptions. At Washington School the secretary would not call the classrooms through the intercom before 10:30 a.m., when "reading time" ended. This contrasted with the situation at another school where teachers were continuously interrupted by intercom messages reminding them to send children to the nurse, counselor, speech therapist, or anyone else in the vicinity of the office.

What the Secretaries Would Rather Not Do

In spite of their willingness to be "Janes of all trades," most school secretaries have their aversions. I tried to find out about these by asking each of the secretaries whether there were any tasks she believed should not be her responsibility.

At first, Edna Brown responded that she was unable to think of any, but when asked specifically about babysitting and first aid, two situations about which many school secretaries have been heard to complain, she expressed her displeasure. She reported that sometimes a teacher would send a child to the office when Mr. John was not there, so she had to attend to the child. She said that she usually called the teacher to explain that the principal was not available, but the teachers were not always willing to take the student back.

Edna reported that parents also sometimes dropped off their children too early so that they ended up sitting in the office for a while. She did not like to be forced to watch the children and often tried to reach the parents by telephone, but that was not always possible.

Edna also disliked taking care of first aid. She said that until recently an excellent nurse had been assigned to the school so she herself had not had much to do with nursing care. Now, she said, she will take a temperature or take care of other minimal necessities if she has to, but she would rather not.

Kathy Orange also mentioned babysitting when asked about tasks she ended up doing that she did not think she should be doing. She referred to day-care center pick-ups that were consistently late. She reported that this problem was a common one and that every afternoon she had "primary students running through [the] office" for 45 minutes. I had observed this situation and the time Kathy had to devote to keeping order among 5 to 10 bored primary-level children with nothing to do. Fortunately the schedule difference that contributed to this problem was corrected that year.

Not all of the interviewed secretaries had problems assuming first-aid responsibilities. Sandy Pink, for example, saw no problem in this except that she thought it silly that she was not allowed to give medication to a child and had to call in a nurse from another school to administer medicine.

She did object, however, to being saddled with discipline problems in the office. Fortunately Mr. Rutherford insisted that children were not to be sent to the office for disciplinary reasons when he was not there unless they were being sent home. This action by the principal relieved her of that responsibility.

Mary Lime was quick to respond to my query about responsibilities she thought ought not to be hers, "Nursing. I really feel strongly about that." She added that everyone was concerned about after-school care but that they seemed less concerned about the health care during the school day. She said, "the school nurse is one of the important medical advisers in the community. They depend on them so many times." She added that parents sometimes would bring children to the school to see if they needed stitches, to check their ears, and for general advice. She thought that if everyone believed after-school care was so important, then there should also be a full-time nurse in the school.

The strong response from someone who was typically soft in voice and manner led me to ask her why she felt so strongly about this. Mary answered that she did not feel competent. "If I had wanted to be a nurse . . ." and she laughed before completing the sentence. Then she related that during the fall term, a boy had suffered a severe asthma attack and died in the school. The health aide had just left when this happened and it was up to the principal and the secretary to take care of the emergency.

Mary argued that more and more children with physical problems were enrolled in the school and that this fact added to her concern. She recalled a boy who had only one artery. The mother said he could do anything, but the child would sometimes "literally turn blue." This often frightened her and the staff.

Her principal, Ms. Alonso, was equally emphatic in her response to the same question. "I don't think she ought to be a nurse." She said she personally took the responsibility for giving medication when the nurse was not there, but if she [the principal] was not there, it fell on Mary's shoulders. She added that it was hard for her to say there was something that the secretary was doing that she should not be doing because "There's so many things. . .so many functions of a school secretary. There's only one person in the office." But she had brought the matter of nursing care to the district and had referred to the case of the boy who died in the school as evidence of that need.

Thus secretaries and their principals were in agreement about both the multiplicity of tasks devolved on the school secretary by virtue of her location in the school and the lack of alternative solutions. Most of them also shared a distaste for at least two tasks that are commonly performed by the school secretary: first-aid and baby-sitting. Responses to the survey, and the perceptions expressed by secretaries and their principals, confirmed the variety of tasks performed by the school secretary and the relative importance of the human aspects of the job. In contrast, the official job descriptions emphasized secretarial tasks and underemphasized the human aspects of the school secretaries' job.

THE HUB OF THE WHEEL

The secretary's position in the physical and operational center of the school placed extraordinary demands on her time and effort. There was no escaping the telephone calls and visitors that streamed through the school office all day and, during the principal's absence from the office, the secretary was the only one available to provide answers (Wolcott, 1973). Two roles were thrust upon her as a result: information center and decision maker.

Information Center

The secretary's role as information center seemed to be the one most demanding of her time and also central to the operation of the school. School secretaries appeared to be repositories for two types of information: current and historical. As a repository of current information, the secretary was the center for receiving and sending information within and beyond the school. The secretary also retained fragments of information while in the process of untangling or clarifying a complex situation. One principal likened the secretary's role to a switchboard, a metaphor that may sound mechanistic, yet effectively captures the reality as observed.

School staff used the secretary as the communication center. She acted as a relay. They brought information to her and she would pass it along to someone else when the opportunity arose. Some secretaries used notes to help them to do this efficiently. Diane Green kept a log of all the messages that came in, highlighting those things she herself had to get done. She explained that she wrote everything in the log and checked it through the day to make sure everything was done. She would put a mark by each entry as soon as the information was passed on or acted upon and said, "I try to [check the book] before the end of the day so we don't miss anything."

Some secretaries made a deliberate effort to be informed. Elsie Lavender confided that she was glad to do typing for the teachers because that way "I'll know what's going on." She explained that the teachers had too many things on their minds and would forget to tell her things. Typing their letters and reports kept her informed.

Mary Lime kept a log of all messages for the principal. The principal checked it routinely and followed up as necessary. She also kept a notebook with all communications sent to parents, whether from the district or from the school, whether routine or individual communication.

At Grant School, Elsie Lavender used a box mounted on the door of the principal's office to deliver all incoming messages. She also placed every message for staff in the appropriate mailbox, folding the paper in such a way that it was readily noticeable by the teacher.

Parents asked for clarifications, sent messages, and sometimes expressed their concerns through the secretary. A student's mother came to ask Diane Green if it was true that her daughter needed to buy school supplies. The secretary explained that everything students needed was provided for them, but perhaps the girl wanted to buy pencils inscribed with the school's name. She also took the opportunity to remind the parent that "the teacher would always be happy to talk to you."

Messages from parents to students came in several times daily. The secretaries relayed the messages or took the necessary steps to change bus assignments, ensure a child would get a lunch when lunch money was forgotten, or smooth out any number of similar situations.

Students would also use the secretary as a relay for messages. One boy spent about 10 minutes one day explaining to Mary Lime how his glasses had been lost and he needed a replacement. He had heard the Lion's Club would provide replacements and asked the secretary to intervene. She promised to let the nurse know so she could make the proper arrangements for him. Another child came at the end of November to complain to Mary that, although she had been entitled to one, she had never received her perfect attendance certificate last year. Mary explained that the teacher she had last year was out but that she would relay the message and "we'll talk about it."

Standard messages were the easier type of information to handle. More difficult were the strings of information that involved several steps and as many participants. In handling these cases secretaries acted more like data banks.

One day two children approached Diane Green. They said their teacher sent them to the office because Johnny was supposed to go to Sue's house after school but Johnny didn't bring a note from home as required. The secretary called Johnny's home but there was no answer. The children explained that was why he was supposed to go to the other house; his father would not be home when the boy arrived there. The secretary tried Sue's house but again, no one was home. She then looked for a work phone for either parent and called Johnny's father at work, but she could not locate him. She tried Sue's mother, who could not come to the phone but got the message and called back. A few minutes later it was confirmed that Johnny was to go to Sue's house that afternoon.

Another even more complicated example occurred when the mother of a newly registered child wanted the girl to be transported to an address outside of the district. After several phone calls, Kathy Orange learned that the address originally given for the child was that of an aunt who lived within the district but that, in fact, the girl lived in a neighboring district. Then the principal had to be involved about whether or not the child would be allowed to stay. The secretary also had to explain all this to the mother and get her to come in to see the principal. The teacher also had to be involved because there was a question about whether or not the girl needed a bilingual classroom that would not be available in the other school. The untangling of this situation, and its final resolution took several days. Throughout the whole process, Kathy was the only repository of all the information. She held the pieces of the puzzle. She spoke to the mother; she then told the principal what the mother had said and vice versa. She also communicated with the district's transportation office as well as with the girl's teacher and with the secretary at the other school who, we might presume, was communicating with her own school staff about the situation.

Historical Information

Another type of information held by the school secretary may be called historical and is similar to the "esoteric organizational knowledge" Vinnicombe (1980) said was held by business secretaries. The school secretary was the one who could answer: "How did we do it last year?" She also remembered former students and teachers. A long-distance phone call came into Dewey School one day. Edna Brown answered and frowned as she tried to place the caller. She then started to smile and answered that the principal was not there but that, yes, she would give him the message. As soon as she got off the telephone, she went to search the files. A few seconds later she triumphantly pulled out a folder and said, "That's it. This is the boy. I thought I recognized him." The long-distance phone call had been from a former student now living in another state. When the principal came to the office she showed him the folder as she gave him the message, reminding him, "You know, he was the one who . . . ."

The secretary in the elementary school office performs many functions, but her role as information center appears to be among the most critical. Although not listed in the job descriptions, her ability to save and pass on pieces of information, to remember and deliver them to the appropriate persons—sometimes after several days, to connect bits gathered from here and there and make sense of them, to retain historical records, and to maintain contacts with outsiders, is taken for granted. And yet it is likely that the value of a secretary to an elementary school principal hinges to a large degree on her ability to perform this function efficiently. These findings echo Evans' (1987) findings at Midstate Hospital. She noted how the institution's clerical workers served as a translation point between the bureaucratic and the organic segments of the organization. Their work, like that of the school secretaries, also remains unacknowledged.

Decision Maker

The secretaries interviewed did not appear eager to make decisions for the principal. Elsie Lavender was clear on this point: "I find that whenever he's gone for one or two or three days, the buck stops with me, and I don't want the buck to stop with me. I want to be able to pass it on to someone else." That is not always possible for the elementary school secretary, as Edna Brown found out one day.

It was time for lunch at the church hall where the school was temporarily housed. The milk delivery had not arrived but kindergartners were lined up waiting to be served. The buses that would take them back to their home school waited outside. In the school's temporary quarters the schedule was tighter than usual; the same buses had to pick up the afternoon students back at the school. The principal was not at the school, and the counselor, who often served as his assistant, was also unavailable. Should the lunch be served without the milk or should they continue to wait? Everyone turned to Edna for a decision. She resisted, but ultimately there was no one else to make a decision and she gave the go-ahead as she muttered under her breath, "I don't get paid for this."

One afternoon at Fillmore School a student ran in to tell Kathy Orange that there was no one outside doing bus duty (supervising students during dismissal). Kathy checked the schedule and found that the music teacher was supposed to be outside. She looked for him but could not locate him. She called a classroom and asked the teacher to send her aide outside. A teacher who happened to be in the office volunteered and Kathy asked the nurse to join them commenting, "That's three. I think they can do it"

There were many other such instances where the secretary had to take immediate action and did so, even if unwillingly. These examples and other such situations did not entail major life and death decisions, but they did impinge on the safety of the students and on the smooth operation of the school.

Rimer (1984) who calls the elementary school secretary an "informal decision maker," relates how during a rainy day when the principal was out of the building, a teacher asked the secretary whether the students should go out for recess or remain inside. He notes that the teachers respect and generally do not question decisions that come from the office. Indeed, his example and the one previously mentioned pertaining to Edna Brown, suggest that teachers may expect, and sometimes even demand, decisive action from the secretary.

Some of those situations arise during times when the principal is not present even though, officially, there would be a teacher-in-charge. Those teachers are not always knowledgeable about relevant policies, as the two secretaries I interviewed in preparation for the study explained.

For example, if a fire alarm rings in the building, even if it is known to be false, fire safety policies demand that students be evacuated from the building. A teacher in charge may not be aware of this policy and might be inclined to ignore an obviously false alarm, especially if the weather is bad or if it is otherwise inconvenient. The secretary would need to inform the teacher of this policy in order to satisfy district requirements.

In another situation, a parent might insist on taking a child home, a reasonable request unless the parent is under court order to stay away from the child. Again the school secretary, not the teacher-in-charge, would have that information in the absence of the principal.

This problem was discussed during a secretaries' meeting I attended in District 2 while conducting the study. One of the secretaries related how a child's father had come to pick her up but only the mother's name was listed as authorized to do so on the "tracer" card. The secretary called the mother, who approved the request, and released the girl to the father. A few days later, the father returned and said his daughter was being transferred to another district. The secretary told him to come back in the afternoon and she would have the transfer papers ready. In the meantime she called the mother, who denied the girl was being transferred. By the time the father returned the mother had picked up the girl. The secretary explained the policy to the father and then also "had a nice talk about stability for the girl" and suggested they "get their act together." Following that discussion, Sandy Pink, with whom I had attended the meeting, told me that problems of custody were her biggest concern.

The secretary's decisions are, of course, not always acceptable. Elsie's decision to move the student in response to his parent's request, previously discussed in detail, is one example. In that case, as in many others, the secretaries weathered the conflict with the principal's support. Their knowledge of that support gave them the security to proceed when necessary. This need was clearly stated by one secretary: "What do I want from my principal? Be supportive, even when I don't do the job well; support me publicly . . . tell me privately that I didn't do the job well" (Sweeney, 1987). The secretaries in this study echoed these sentiments.

FOUR

The Secretary and the Principal

SEEING EYE TO EYE

The secretary and the principal are most often the only two people in the school office. They are also highly dependent on each other. The principal is the main, if not the only, evaluator of the secretary's work. And the principal depends on the secretary to connect with all the various clients served by the school. In conducting this research I was particularly interested in how the relationship between the principal and the secretary was established and maintained. The data for this chapter were derived from the survey, the observations, and the interviews.

General Characteristics of the Relationship

The secretary's relationship with the principal varied a great deal from school to school. All the secretaries observed and interviewed spoke well of their principals. They noted the principal's accomplishments: "He won the faculty over with love," "She's extremely well organized," "She gets *everyone* involved." They also spoke of the principal's support: "He went after that teacher because he thought she made me cry," or "It wouldn't have been her decision but she supported me."

In the survey the secretaries also rated their principals very highly. They gave them the highest ratings for friendliness. Although they ranked them slightly lower in leadership, they still placed them at the upper end of the scale in that quality.

The school offices where this research was conducted were all identified as "good settings." It is not surprising, then, that in their comments to the researcher, principals and secretaries almost always spoke of each other in admiring and respectful terms. At no time during the observations were a principal or secretary observed expressing anger to their complement; nor were they ever heard to complain about each other in public.

The closest to a complaint was from Edna Brown. During the time the school was temporarily located at the church site, she wanted very much to be in "her office." The principal, however, wanted her at the church site. She expressed her frustration in a plaintive voice: "I *don't know* why he wants me here." She did not elaborate. Most of the time she blamed the workers and the school district staff for the frustrating situation.

Little joking and/or overt expressions of affection were observed between the principals and their secretaries. The one exception occurred at Washington School. It was noted earlier that the teachers there tended to congregate in a small room near the secretary's desk. The principal's office was also nearby. This arrangement and the close quarters appeared to encourage informal interactions among the staff, including the principal and the secretary.

The easy bantering and light humor between the Washington School principal and the secretary, and between both of them and the rest of the staff was not typical. This is not to say that there was a total absence of humor at the other sites. Rather, in most school offices the general tone of the interactions between the secretary and the principal was observed to be businesslike and task oriented, although humorous situations did surface at times. The forced intimacy of the small office at Washington may have contributed to the easy-going atmosphere. It may also be that the shared experience of opening a new school, and the shared discomforts that situation entailed had contributed to closer relationships among the staff.

Table 4.1 Secretaries' Rankings of the Types of Assistance They Offer Principals

Task	Mode	Mean
Keeping Records	1.0	3.2
Providing Support	1.0	3.6
Providing Information	2.0	3.0
Attending to Problems During His/Her Absence	3.0	3.8
Screening Calls	6.0	4.8
Keeping Calendar	7.0	5.4
Screening Visitors	7.0	5.4
Giving Advice	8.0	6.8

On a scale where 1 is the most frequently occurring activity and 8 the least frequently occurring.

Contributions to the Principal's Work

The secretaries responding to the survey were asked to assess their contribution to the principal's work by ranking eight items according to their perception of how their assistance was most helpful to the principal (see Table 4.1). The three tasks through which they said they could be especially helpful to the school principal were keeping records, providing information, and providing support. Among these, providing information received the highest ranking overall, a process that, as described in the previous section, tends to be carried out through informal, daily interactions rather than through formal meetings.

During her interview Elsie Lavender stated her primary responsibility clearly: "to make sure the school runs as smoothly and as effectively as possible." When asked to explain, she talked about making sure that messages sent to the teachers were clear, that the calendar changed as little as possible, and that the school day had as few interruptions as possible. She added that the principal would sometimes ask her opinion about certain activities and sometimes heeded her advice. She gave several examples, all of which related to her concern about overburdening teachers. She differentiated her contribution from "squealing" because she said that when she and the principal first started to work together, he told her to feel free to come in and talk, that he wanted to know all that was going on in the school.

Kathy Orange also believed that her major contribution to Fillmore School's principal was to provide information. She did this by getting him the data he needed for different purposes. She had also "discovered . . . different ways of handling parents" in order to get from them information that "will help us place the children better."

Sharing Information with the Principal

Although communication between the principal and the secretary was most usually carried out through informal interactions, these interactions occurred frequently and appeared to satisfy the need for close contact between them. The secretary's usefulness as a conduit of information to the principal was observed often and mentioned frequently during the interviews.

At Grant School, a newly-hired nurse behaved in a manner deemed irresponsible by the secretary and other members of the staff. As Elsie Lavender reported,

> She came in here . . . she didn't like filing . . . and then she didn't like doing all the paperwork . . . . And everytime we turned around she was in the lounge having a cigarette. She was never here when kids came along needing help . . . . She had seen children with lice and sent them back to the classroom for the teacher to take care of it, and she had seen children with chickenpox and sent *them* back . . . no communication at all with the teachers.

The critical incident occurred when a substitute teacher at the school fell and hurt her ankle. Elsie called the nurse who responded by asking her to tell an aide. But Elsie responded, "No, you go there and take care of that teacher." By this time the teacher had been brought to the office and the nurse put a bandage on her and left. Not knowing what to do next, one of the teachers went to ask the nurse what they should do and was told by her to call the district office. But, as Elsie told it, "I said, no way, and that's when I got on the intercom and called [the nurse] and said you need to come and take care of Dolores and call the district."

The nurse continued to break the rules by delegating to the clerical aide and failing to communicate, as required, with the health aide assigned as her partner and with the district office. Throughout these events the principal had not been involved in the case. After a few days, Elsie went to Mr. Ulysses and said, "I don't know what all the teachers have said to you, and I don't know what, if anything, [the health aide] has said. I got a complaint about the nurse." She then proceeded to relate the events of the past few days. The principal had not heard any complaints from anyone else, but he called the school with which they shared the service and sure enough, they had problems too. Shortly thereafter the nurse was dismissed from her job.

Most of the time the secretary's function as conduit of information for the principal was less dramatic. It was actually so pervasive as to be hardly noticeable. It was the teacher coming to the secretary and asking her to tell the principal whatever was on his or her mind at the time. It was the custodian asking the secretary to relay to the principal that the boys in the west wing had again stopped the toilets.

Sometimes there was happy information to relay. At Washington School, in an effort to get students to return their emergency cards promptly (cards filled out by the parents with information about whom and where to contact a relative or friend in case of an emergency), the principal offered a reward to the class that would be first to get all emergency cards back. Later the secretary would excitedly announce the winning class to the principal and animatedly describe the furious but friendly competition that had followed her announcement of the contest.

Secretaries also were often the first to hear about someone's intention to retire or transfer. Sometimes they were asked to tell the principal, as was the case with the custodian of one school. By the time she had told the principal, Diane had also started preparations for a proper farewell from the staff. At other times secretaries heard the news first because the teacher or staff member needed to know appropriate procedures or to secure required forms, as in the case of a transfer.

Formal Communication

Sixty percent of the secretaries surveyed said they never participated in regularly scheduled meetings with their principals. Those who reported meeting with their principals regularly reported meeting periods ranging from as little as 10 minutes per week to as much as 8 hours per week. Most said they met with their principals for one-half hour per week.

This pattern was also observed at the schools. Some secretaries had many, often lengthy, interactions with the principal daily. Some exchanged very few words with them. But only one principal and his secretary held weekly scheduled meetings.

The principal-secretary team at Hayes School met every Monday morning to review their plans for the week. Meetings lasted about 2 hours and followed a mutually-agreed-upon agenda. The nurse was asked to answer the telephone and take messages while the secretary was at the meeting. This precaution minimized but did not totally eliminate interruptions. The secretary sometimes had to leave the meeting to attend to a newly registering family or to answer a question from a teacher. Less often the principal might be beckoned to the telephone or a teacher might insist on seeing him; however, everyone tried to avoid distractions.

Monday meetings at Hayes School were used to discuss upcoming events, such as the celebration of the state's birthday, Student Council activities, Parent-Teacher Organization activities, the principal's and the secretary's calendars, and progress reports on various activities such as the secretary's use of a new computer program. Items of a more personal nature, such as a teacher's illness or the death of a teacher's family member, were also discussed at these meetings. The secretary also took advantage of the Monday meetings to prod the principal to complete the required number of fire drills or to move forward the plans for the state birthday celebrations.

The secretary at Hayes, Sandy Pink, was more involved than most in peripheral activities where she acted as the principal's surrogate. These activities included, for example, the United Way fund-raising drive or the Student Council. At the weekly meetings she would report to the principal about her participation in these activities and their outcome.

During these meetings Sandy acted as an administrative assistant. She contributed her ideas, reported on the progress of ongoing activities, reminded the principal of neglected commitments, and shared in the planning for future activities. Most of the follow-up required after the meeting was handled by Sandy Pink. She had a system whereby she immediately wrote out pertinent notes directing necessary action. For example, if the principal needed to see teachers X, Y, and Z, she wrote a brief note to each of them during the meeting. At the end of the meeting she put these notes in the teachers' mailboxes. During the meeting she also made notes directly on her calendar about the principal's activities and sometimes added notes to his calendar as well.

Informal Communication

The situation at Hayes School was not typical. It is emphasized here because the system appeared to be mutually satisfying and efficient. In most schools interactions between the secretary and the principal were usually brief and to the point. Secretaries tended to answer specific questions from the principal or to relay specific messages. These exchanges usually took place near the secretary's desk. In most cases, the principal would come to the secretary's desk and make a specific request; for example, "Would you tell Ms. Jones that I need to see her today?" The secretary would generally seize the opportunity to give the principal a message or to pass on some information: "Alice called; she says they will be able to pick up Sally (a new student) at the corner beginning tomorrow." As the principal moved on, the secretary would attempt to contact Ms. Jones, either through the intercom or by leaving a message in her mailbox. Unless the principal indicated otherwise, the secretary would usually stop whatever she was doing to take care of the principal's request first.

Most principals had an open-door policy, but while the secretaries might go in and out of the principal's office many times during the day, they did not often spend extended periods of time there. Secretaries complained that if a teacher appeared at the door while they were speaking to the principal, the teacher was given preference.

At Washington School, the proximity of the secretary's desk to the principal's office and desk appeared to contribute to more frequent and general interactions. While sitting at her desk, the principal would make a comment to the secretary as she went through her mail. The secretary, also at her desk, would respond, and they would engage in a brief conversation. The principal, Ms. George, was more likely than her colleagues to ask the secretary to come into her office to plan an upcoming activity or task together. In these cases she would ask for and receive the secretary's opinion.

The secretary at Dewey School was the only one who used shorthand. The principal, Mr. John, told me that he found dictation very useful. He said it provided him with the opportunity to think through what he was saying and that he liked to have Edna Brown react to the content as she was taking it down. However, while I was often present during dictation, I never heard Edna make any comments to the principal about the content of what he was dictating. The principal would sometimes ask questions or make comments, but Edna would only nod or smile in response. Her reaction suggested that she did not really want to know what she did not need to know. On the other hand, his comments did not appear designed to encourage dialogue. For example, while he was dictating his negative evaluation of a teacher he commented, " I don't like doing this but I don't have any choice."

Shared Perceptions

We might assume that the extent of shared perceptions is likely to affect the close, interdependent relationship between principal and secretary in the elementary school. Several questions during the interviews were directed at tapping the level of compatibility that existed between principals and their secretaries. Principals and secretaries were asked to describe the school community, to identify problems, and to describe each other's jobs. Their responses were then compared to find out the similarity of their responses. The similarity, or level of compatibility, varied across schools, although all were found to be very compatible. But even among these, the high compatibility in the responses offered by the principal and the secretary at Washington School were unusual.

The principal and the secretary at Washington used almost identical language to describe the school environment and its clientele. Most characteristic of their descriptions was the use of the terms "caring," "closeness," and "small."

Secretary: We're small and we have a little more time than other schools. There's just a very, very unique closeness there.
Principal: Because we're small, we think we're a little bit unique. I think it holds us together even more.

The adjective "special" was also used by both secretary and principal when referring to the school:

Secretary: It's just so very special at this school.
Principal: It's really special.

Principal and secretary also expressed similar priorities regarding the school secretary's position:

Principal: Someone . . . that could really be supportive and positive.
Secretary: It's a position of serving the needs of others.

The fact that principal and secretary expressed similar expectations for the school secretary was not surprising in this case. The principal acknowledged during her interview that when she applied for the job at Washington, she decided that if she got the job she would encourage Diane to apply for the secretary's position. The principal had been a teacher at a school where Diane had been the office clerk. Her expectations for the secretary were "to have someone just like Diane." The qualities she sought and that Diane exemplified were for someone who was "organized, could complete a task, could maintain a pleasant demeanor, was bright, kind of creative . . . a good typist." She added that at first Diane's typing skills "were not the greatest" but she was willing to forego those in favor of human relations skills. The former, she said, could be developed, while the later "is something innate."

Diane and her principal also shared similar expectations for the principal. Diane emphasized the importance of having any boss be in control: "Everybody wants to have a boss, whether it's the principal of the school or the manager of the finance company, that you feel is in control."

Her principal used different language but also emphasized the importance of being in control when she described the principal as the one who "keeps all the balls in the air."

At Dewey School the principal and the secretary both described the school in relation to its ethnic composition, socioeconomic status (SES), and the low schooling level of the families in the school community:

Secretary: The main thing is the ethnic background . . . the real poverty in our particular area.
Principal: What makes it unique is our population, almost 87% Hispanic . . . a very low socioeconomic situation.

Both emphasized the parents' lack of schooling and how this prevented them from offering adequate support and from participating as fully as possible in school activities.

Kathy Orange and Mr. Millard both described Fillmore School as very large and having an economically and racially balanced student population. He described it as a "melting pot."

The secretary of Grant School, Elsie, described the school in terms of its student population's transient, low socio-economic status: "very underprivileged . . . the underdog of the world." Mr. Ulysses expressed mildly different perceptions about the school. But he also called it "a very good school," particularly in the services provided the minority population. He noted that few students arrived in school prepared to learn but emphasized that within 2 to 3 years they were achieving at some of the highest levels in the district.

At Alvarez School, secretary Mary Lime, suggested the school was like a family: "Anything that hurts one hurts them all." She believed the faculty was "unusual," with none of the "cliques" that affect other schools. She also emphasized the cooperation of the parents: "I've never seen such work in the school as these parents do." She reported that some even called her and came in during the summer to help her get ready for the opening of school; and said that a large number of volunteers helped the teachers in the classroom regularly.

In spite of her brief tenure at Alvarez School, Ms. Alonso also emphasized the quality of "closeness" among the school faculty: "They're a very close-knit faculty, very supportive . . . of each other," and "of students and parents alike." She called it, "one of the nicest situations I've ever been in."

Insofar as these principals and secretaries were concerned, a high level of mutual respect and appreciation was expressed in the school office. In addition, these secretaries and their principals appear to share similar perceptions about their schools; they see "eye to eye."

INDUCTING THE ADMINISTRATOR

Results from the survey indicate that, while principals come and go, secretaries remain in the same school for many years. A newly appointed principal is thus likely to begin his or her career in the company of an experienced secretary. The asymmetrical relationship between an experienced secretary and a neophyte principal raises some interesting issues related to the principals' induction into the job.

Among the secretaries interviewed, three had preceded their principals at the school and three had been hired by the current principal. All of them were asked how they might handle the arrival of a new principal at the school. Their principals also were asked their expectations for the secretary when they moved to a new school.

Most of the secretaries emphasized the need to get to know what the new principal wants and how they want to have things done. Diane Green said she would expect to spend a lot of time talking with the new person to build a good line of communication. She saw her role as being sensitive to the new person's priorities since new principals were likely to have their own ideas about what is important. She would emphasize communication and would expect the principal to communicate his or her needs. She would want that principal to be available to answer her many questions about expectations and priorities.

Ms. George, her principal, also emphasized communication and the sharing of expectations. She would like to know what the secretary had been used to doing and to develop "a close relationship" by clearly defining her own expectations as well as listening to what the secretary expected from her.

If a different principal were assigned to Dewey School, Edna Brown stated that she would first familiarize that person with the way office procedures had been carried out in the past. She would then want to know if that was the way the new principal wanted to proceed. She would not continue doing something "her way" just because that was the way she had always done it. However, she added that she would try to convince a new person to use her procedure if she had found a particularly effective way of doing something.

As an established secretary receiving a new principal, Kathy Orange said she would offer to answer questions on recent events at the school in order to help the new person get oriented. She would also pass on information about the parents—especially how they might be handled—but would be careful what she would say about the teachers. New principals, she said, "have to develop their own means of working with teachers."

Mr. Millard indicated that he would want to start off with a new secretary by developing a personal relationship and by striving for an understanding and appreciation of each other. He would then adapt the job to the new secretary's skills and experiences, knowing that this might force him to accept some responsibilities previously delegated to an experienced secretary.

If she were to receive a new principal, Elsie Lavender said she would do just what she did for Mr. Ulysses. He arrived at the school with no experience at the elementary school level, so she discussed with him everything regarding the opening of school. She also tried to be available to answer his questions although that meant she sometimes had to work late or take her own work home to complete it.

Mr. Ulysses said he would first like to sit down with the established secretary and go over all the routines that had been in operation, "so you don't look like you're walking around with your head in the clouds." He said he would want the secretary to make him aware of any special aspects of the curriculum, things "everybody is proud of," because he would not want to tamper with those. The secretary could also orient him to the community and to work relationships and perhaps even suggest some changes. An inexperienced principal, Mr. Ulysses said, would benefit particularly from an experienced secretary's help in arranging daily and weekly schedules. He thought new administrators needed to rely on their secretaries "almost as their assistant."

Sandy Pink explained that she had struggled with this question the previous summer. Before district administrators decided to transfer her along with Mr. Rutherford to Hayes School, she was expecting a new, inexperienced principal at her former school. Concerned about how this person was going to be prepared for the position, she called the district office and asked, "Who trains Ms. X to be a principal?" The answer was, "nobody." Sandy arrived immediately at the logical conclusion, "You mean it's me? I'm the one?" She then tried to make contact with the principal-to-be in order to get some forms ready for the opening of school and prepare the staff handbook. Fortunately "a weight was lifted off my shoulders" when she was asked to move to Hayes with Mr. Rutherford. She reasoned, "It was like I was training her . . . and who was I to train her?"

Sandy could also recall Mr. Rutherford's arrival at her former school and how she had helped him. She recalled discussing with him the strong points of certain teachers, facilitating his assigning them to specific tasks.

Mr. Rutherford pointed out that one of Sandy's advantages was knowing the idiosyncrasies of teachers, the "culture of relationships." She had helped him, he said, by sharing that knowledge so that he could approach his staff in the most effective and timely manner.

Sandy said she believed she could "contribute a lot to bridging the gap . . . and bridging with parents that I already knew." She added that it was much easier for him because she had already learned about many situations that would have been difficult for him to learn on his own. Sandy also explained to Mr. Rutherford how things had been done in the past. As a result of that help, he was able to modify his expectations at the beginning in order to avoid direct conflict with established routines. She said, "He came in like a whirlwind and it was my job . . . to calm him down."

Mary Lime supposed she would need to start with the basics, particularly with someone who had no administrative experience at all. Although Ms. Alonso, her current principal, was an experienced principal, Mary had helped her to become familiar with District 2's policies and with the routines already established at Alvarez School.

Ms. Alonso, who had only recently experienced the situation to which she was responding, noted that she would like the established secretary to orient her to the school, to how and what things were done. She would want to know about the history of the school and about its traditions. In this way, as a new principal, she could avoid disrupting too many important things too fast.

The principal at Mary Lime's school also recognized that the secretary was privy to information to which the principal had no, or only limited, access. She explained that this was particularly the case when the principal was new to the community. Ms. Alonso suggested that the secretary could help the principal in these situations by alerting her to particular concerns and by helping her to gain knowledge about the staff and community.

Thus it is that elementary school secretaries participate in the induction of new principals. They share historical information and their huge store of knowledge about routines. They also familiarize the newcomer with the district and community, and provide a bridge that facilitates the faculty's acceptance of the new principal. In their responses, these secretaries appeared cautious. They did not want to overstep their boundaries. They wanted to know what the new principal wanted, and were ready to change their behavior to suit the principal.

The principals, for their part, seemed well aware of their secretary's value as a repository of useful information and as an experienced and trusted member of the staff. Their responses were not too different from those of the secretaries. As newly appointed principals they would want from the secretaries the same help the secretaries were willing to offer.

The induction of principals has been described as a "sink or swim" process. Principals are typically placed in their new positions and expected to become instant leaders with minimal help from their district (Anderson, 1988). The role of the secretary as the inductor of new principals is never mentioned in this literature, yet their contribution is readily acknowledged by principals. The role is also ignored in the official job descriptions that suggest instead an all-knowing principal who gives the orders and a subordinate secretary who carries them out. It is curious that, as Sandy Pink found out, this unassigned task, like so many others, defaults to the school secretary. This raises a question worthy of further research. To what extent is the principal's success related to the effectiveness of the training the secretary provides?

ISSUES OF GENDER

Within the constellation of factors that affect women's career choices, the position of elementary school secretary emerges as one that fulfills most of the characteristics for a job suited to females. School secretaries work with children within schedules compatible with the family schedule. They perform tasks similar to the social maintenance and housekeeping responsibilities of wives and mothers—from keeping track of appointments and correspondence to administering first aid. Most school secretaries also work for a male principal. In this respect they may fit into the role of "office wives," much as their colleagues in business do.

As previously noted, the six secretaries and their principals observed in their school offices were also interviewed for this study. As I analyzed their responses to the questions, the difference between male and female responses became apparent. In this section I will compare the responses to the interview questions given by the four male principals and their secretaries to those of the two female principals and their secretaries.

Perceptions About the Secretary's Job

The six principals interviewed emphasized similar aspects of their secretaries' work. They all spoke of the central position occupied by the secretary, of the secretary as the school (and their) representative, of the support she offered the principal, and of her role as conduit of information. The secretaries emphasized the same aspects of their jobs, but their self-appraisals tended to be more modest than the principals' appraisals.

Male and female principals differed in the attention they devoted to each of these aspects of the secretary's job. Male principals placed a major emphasis on the centrality of the position, on the representational role, and on the secretary's support. Female principals put more emphasis on the secretary's role as a conduit of information, particularly information that did not move through official channels, such as comments made during casual conversation.

Male and female principals also differed in their descriptions of the secretary-principal relationship. Male principals relied on a marriage metaphor. Female principals relied on a model that may best be described as collegial. That is, they put their emphasis on shared work. Interestingly, the secretaries' responses tended to be similar to those of their principals. Secretaries who worked for a male principal relied on marriage or mothering metaphors, while those who worked for a female principal described a collegial relationship.

She's Always There

The school secretary sits at both the physical and the operational center of the school. One of the male principals noted, "the convenience of her being there . . . at all times, behind her desk, behind the counter. She's *always* there. People will always come to her first." As a result, the secretary often ends up performing tasks that might be more properly assigned to the principal. One principal commented, "There are a number of things that may fall into my domain . . . but because she happens to be there, she has to make a decision."

The convenience of the secretary's central location also poses a danger, as expressed by another male principal: "Some . . . find themselves in the position of running the school on a daily basis by the nature of where they're sitting."

All agree that the central position occupied by the secretary requires enormous flexibility. It also requires the ability to handle many situations simultaneously. This ability was particularly emphasized by the four male principals. One of them proudly described his secretary's ability to "handle a number of professionals at one time . . . . She can have six things going on . . . and still maintain calm composure and focus on whatever is going on." Another male principal referred to his secretary as "the calm in the eye of the storm."

The secretaries interviewed tended to take the demands of their job and their skills in stride: "Basically it's just being there and taking care of the problems and things as they come in." Another secretary, when asked if she sometimes ended up doing things that were not her responsibility, responded as follows:

> I've done everything imaginable and none of it seems like it should be somebody else's responsibility. And if it even was, at the time the other person whose responsibility it was, was not available to do it, and somebody has to do it, so . . . .

A Very Good Ambassador

The central position occupied by the secretary is closely allied to principals' perceptions that the secretary represents the school: "I rely heavily on [her] to project the image of [the] school . . . [she] is a very, very good ambassador for the school. People feel comfortable with her and that makes my job a lot simpler."

Another male principal expressed this aspect of the secretary's job in a very personal way: "She represents me. She is me."

The female principals endorsed the secretary's role as school representative, but neither of these principals expressed this aspect of the secretary's job in personal terms. For example, one female principal related the secretary's representation of the school image to the attention she must give to parents: "[You] represent the image of the school, and I expect . . . when a parent comes in you deal with them promptly."

The secretaries interviewed recognized the representational role they played but did not give it a great deal of attention. A comment from one secretary reflects this awareness and also pride in her own performance: "I've parents all the time telling me that they're just real happy they've got a secretary who smiles when they walk in the door."

Head Communicator

In a manner similar to that of the business secretaries studied by Vinnicombe (1980), school secretaries are also at the information center of the school. One principal called her "the head communicator for the whole school" and explained that in selecting a secretary he would "look for somebody bright enough to recognize what's going on as far as the school and its organization is concerned."

This aspect of the secretary's job extends to the reception and interpretation of extra-official information as well. "She picks up information and relays it," said one male principal, again relying on a mechanistic image. Another male commented, "Secretaries are in a very key position to know what's happening in an organization. It's interesting that we don't consult them more."

Female principals did consult them more. These principals seemed to value and utilize the secretary's unique access to information networks. They made many more statements about this aspect of the secretary's job, illustrating their comments with specific cases of when their secretary had been able to provide important information. Ms. Alonso, who had been only recently hired by the district and assigned to her school, still relied on the secretary to cue her about the community and about what she might expect from specific parents. Both female principals also noted that secretaries are viewed as less threatening by the staff and can therefore "catch more off the cuff and informal talk."

All the secretaries were also aware of their position at the crossroads of the school's communication network. One commented proudly on her ability to identify the special needs of students: "I've discovered over the years different ways of handling parents, different ways of digging information out of them that will help place their children better."

The central position occupied by the secretary can also cause difficulties when the secretary ends up in the middle of a conflict between the principal and the teachers. The secretaries who worked with the female principals appeared to be more comfortable in their role as conduits of information. Both of them carefully distinguished between "tattling" or "gossiping" on the one hand, and being what one of them called "a feeler" for the principal on the other. She explained that the latter requires that "you let them know when there's a situation brewing . . . that they need to take care of . . . . You don't have to bring names into it."

A Supportive Role

Principals count on their secretaries for support. Male principals were more likely to link support to assistance given to them personally, someone who will "take the load off of me . . . so that I could spend more time concentrating on nonroutine decision making and organization."

Another male principal was even more specific. He said he knew his "Jungian personality type" and therefore looked for someone to complement him, someone "who is very steady and is systematic in the way they do things and can keep track of things for me." His current secretary, he says, has those qualities and "plays a very strong supportive role" for him.

For both female principals the need for support appeared to be less personal. They linked this aspect of the secretary's work to specific assistance. For Ms. Alonso, the newly assigned principal, the secretary's support helped her to learn about her new setting in order to act in consonance with it. The other female principal spoke of her secretary's support as an asset for "molding the staff together."

The provision of support is not without problems for the secretaries. They are eager to support their principals, but unsure about where to draw the line. This was a difficult problem for a secretary whose principal sometimes spent part of the school hours in nonschool activities: "I'll just say he's not here right now, and that, I think, has bothered me more than anything. Because, where does your loyalty lie?" She answered her own question unequivocally: "With the boss."

I recalled Rose Marie Wood's behavior as secretary to the President during the Watergate crisis, and my own school secretary's attempt to convince me that such behavior was appropriate for a secretary. But this secretary remained ambivalent: "I don't want to lie to anyone and yet I don't want to get him in trouble. I wouldn't get him into trouble for anything."

Another secretary, who had responded with assurance that her primary responsibility in the school was toward the children, recalled her difficulties with a former principal: "He didn't like children anymore . . . .I could sense it and the parents knew it too . . . . I did a lot of covering up for him . . . trying to smooth it over."

The secretary's support appears to have important benefits for the principals. For the secretaries themselves it can become a source of conflict whenever the principal fails to act honorably. In those situations the secretary may find herself in the middle of a serious moral conflict. Since the principal is also the secretary's chief (and usually only) evaluator, she has to consider not only loyalty, but also the potential threat to her livelihood.

Metaphors and Gender

Traditional role expectations for females echoed in the interview responses of the four male principals and in the responses of their secretaries. In contrast, the responses of the two female principals and their secretaries tended to emphasize a collegial, friendly relationship based on mutual trust. The metaphors chosen by interviewees to describe the secretary-principal relationship are illustrative of these differences.

Marriage

Only one of the male principals interviewed explicitly used marriage as a metaphor to describe the relationship between himself and his secretary: "She and I have to become one. We have to be as far [sic] as committed marriage partners." The same principal offered this advice to school secretaries: "You're gonna marry your boss . . . you're gonna create a marital relationship . . . . Become one in philosophy . . . become one in strategies . . . always be understanding and forgiving . . . . Give support to the principal even when he's wrong."

Other principals were less explicit, but their statements nonetheless strongly suggested traditionally held expectations for wives. For example, one male principal commented that his secretary "screens any negative comment so I don't have to hear it." Another one noted how when making decisions, his secretary was "sharp enough to realize that she has to be timing it so that it's as if you were the person who was in charge totally, and she's making you feel that you're making decisions but she's already on top of it." And the principal whose secretary is covering up for his absences revealed: "I know if I asked anything of her she'd do everything within reason to help me."

Mothering

The responses of the male principals' secretaries also reflected traditional gender roles, but their comments sounded more like those descriptive of mothers than wives. Sometimes the metaphor was explicitly used:

> You have to be a mother to him. You have to take care of him . . . like today, he was freezing . . . [and] here he was drinking this Coke . . . . So I said, "My gosh!, you're gonna get pneumonia." . . . So I went out and made him some tea . . . . I don't do it all the time . . . only whenever he's coming in with an extra burden . . . . I mother him, give him extra attention.

But more often it was implicit: "Now, I've told him a couple of weeks ago, I said: 'Dick [Mr. John], you'd better settle down. You'd better take it easy and not get so upset over a lot of little things.'"

Sometimes the secretaries to these male principals sounded more like compliant wives than competent office managers: "You have to learn to take his temper . . . you know, just bite your tongue and walk away . . . .He'll growl when he's upset, you know . . . " Or:

> I know not to present him with certain things that arrive at a certain time, and you have to determine, well maybe he'll be in a better mood when he comes back from lunch, I'll tell him then . . . . I don't think I need to add to his frustration.

The protection these secretaries provide for their male principals also has its costs. For one secretary the principal's active participation in districtwide activities means assuming responsibilities such as assigning children to classrooms, signing time cards and payroll slips, writing the parents' newsletter, and sometimes even taking

charge of student council. She performed these duties in addition
to her regular clerical duties as the only secretary in a school of 400
students. As a result, "I can't even get my own work done, I'm so
busy helping in these areas."

Sandy Pink cautiously expressed ambivalent feelings about how
her work was affected by the principal's absence from the school
site:

> There were times when disciplining situations would come up
> . . . or a nursing situation . . . and I had to handle some of those
> things and I think a little bit . . . I'd resent his being gone as
> much as he was. And yet . . . I'm proud that I can be the one
> to run it for him so that he can be, y'know, running his
> committees.

There was also ambivalence on the part of the male principals.
But their ambivalence was related to fears of losing control, of
losing power: "She could undermine me fully if she were not
wholly supportive."

In statements that recalled McClure's 1930 warning, these principals would, at one and the same time, praise their secretaries for
their skills in decision making, and then express their concern over
their secretaries' potential for assuming the principal's responsibilities. They seemed to fear the possibility that the secretary might
usurp their position. Thus the principal whose secretary took over
his school duties in order to allow him to participate in committees
described his secretary's role as follows:

> She buys into and operates within the constraints that I've laid
> down. . . .She makes the same decisions that I make. She gets
> a pretty fine script that I write for her. . . . I want her to be
> another me. . . . She has to be very empathetic . . . and feel the
> feelings I do.

Another principal, who had earlier praised his secretary's intel-
ligence and her ability to handle any situation, added,

> What I'm finding out . . . is that everything in the school, not
> everything . . . many things . . . which are depending too much
> on one person. It's Kathy this, and Kathy that, and we run a

risk of being too narrow in our focus . . . and that person becomes so strong in their role that if they weren't there, the place wouldn't operate. So for that reason I think it's important to defuse the responsibility a little.

The same principal would advise an incoming principal that "Kathy can sometimes take the ball out of your court . . . and in trying to be helpful she may go a step too far."

The secretaries of these male principals did not seem to be aware of their concerns. Kathy Orange, for example, seemed to enjoy any opportunity to learn and grow but she was also cognizant of the principal's needs. It was Kathy who noted the need to be careful about when to approach the principal with a problem.

Gender Differences

One might say that these relationships are no different than any other boss-subordinate relationship. The secretaries studied by Kanter (1978) and Vinnicombe (1983), discussed above, behaved in similar fashion. However, neither of those researchers explored the possible interaction of gender in those relationships. What is notable here are the distinct differences among the six principal and secretary teams interviewed for this study. Whereas the marriage and mothering metaphors were rampant in the comments made by male principals *and* their secretaries, those metaphors were *never* used by any member of the two female-female teams.

The statements of female principals and their secretaries were punctuated by terms such as trust, confidence, and teamwork. Male principals never used confidence and/or confidentiality to describe their relationship with the secretaries. Female principals made *no* statements such as those made by the male principals suggesting ambivalence about their secretaries' skills or decision-making power.

One female principal, for example, described how she would choose a secretary by listing five priorities among which the third was trustworthiness: "to hold the confidentiality that is in the office." The other female principal and her secretary made similar statements regarding confidentiality. The principal said, "She knows she can talk to me in confidence. And I know I can talk to her in confidence." Her secretary used almost identical words to express similar feelings: "She knows she can talk to me and her ideas will not go any further. We have a real good relationship."

The secretaries and principals in these pairs used the words "team" and "teamwork" often to refer to the secretary-principal relationship. One secretary explained how "every position in the school staff is serving, and you do it as a team." And one of the female principals addressed the issue of compatibility between the secretary and the principal in the following statement: "You need to make sure you're in the same kind of ballgame with that person you're working with 'cause I don't think you can be at odds with each other. You have to be a real team." It is interesting that the sentiments expressed by this principal were similar to those expressed by one of her male colleagues cited earlier. But he used a marriage metaphor to express what she described with a sports metaphor.

The ambivalence expressed by the male principals and their secretaries appears to be related to the problem of intermittent power mentioned earlier. The secretaries are expected to be loyal executors of the principal's wishes most of the time. But when the principal is unavailable, or when the principal chooses to delegate, the secretary must pick up the slack. The ambiguity of this situation demands extraordinary emotional resources from the secretary who must continually assess a situation in order to give the appropriate response. It is interesting that this problem was not evident in the relationship between the female principals and their secretaries.

Male-female and female-female teams differed in other ways. One of these is in their emphasis on what the two secretaries of the female principals called "consideration." The other is in the degree to which they demonstrated what I have chosen to call "parity" in their relationships.

Consideration

Three of the four secretaries working with male principals complained about last-minute assignments. These assignments were a big problem for them because they added confusion to an already demanding and unpredictable schedule. In addition, they found rushing through a lengthy report or other last-minute tasks extremely difficult to perform in the midst of the constant interruptions that tend to characterize the elementary school office.

In contrast, the two secretaries working with female principals emphasized their boss' "consideration" regarding their work. Both of these women had worked with what one of them called "last-minute people" who, they said, "put a lot of pressure on everybody who works under them." They found their current (female) principals "more organized" and appreciated that they "keep things current." In addition, both secretaries were confident that their female principals minimized their time away from school. And when these principals had to be away from the school site, their secretaries claimed they always knew where to find them: "One of [the principal's] good qualities [is] she's always available."

In both cases, the secretaries of these two female principals also noted that their principals made careful arrangements before expected absences in order to minimize the secretary's load: "We always try to have it so there's someone there with me . . . a nurse or something . . . .She always leaves things covered so that I never have to worry about that."

The same secretary's principal expressed her concern for the secretary's well-being: "She's just so willing to do everything. And sometimes you can take advantage of a person like that. That's why I'm at school from 7:30 a.m. until it closes . . . why I don't leave until she leaves."

She recalled a recent incident when she was away and several children were sent to the office. The secretary had a very difficult time trying to keep them under control while she went about her work. The principal added: "And you know, that's hard . . . . How can you do what you're supposed to do and watch five kids who are misbehaving?"

The female principal's view contrasts with that of her male colleagues, several of whom noted that a good administrator should not be missed because there should be systems in place to cope with these absences: "If I truly am a good administrator, I shouldn't be missed by being absent up to two days a week," said one. He pointed out how his absences were actually good for the secretary:

She is able to exercise more full control because somebody has to pass judgment, and then she can do that . . . and it strengthens her in the eyes of the staff. . . . That's an important variable. The strength of the school rests on whether or not she can do that . . . . If she can't . . . then I can't extend myself into other areas.

Parity

A more elusive characteristic of the relationship between female principals and their secretaries was the sense of parity. I use parity in this context to refer to the comparability that I could sense in the relationship. It was most clearly evident in the responses of principals and secretaries to a question about the problems that might be caused by the secretary's absence. The secretary to one of the female principals did not think her absence would make a lot of difference to the principal because,

I can't imagine a lot of things that she [the principal] couldn't do without me. She knows pretty much where everything is in the office . . . . I have told her on occasion that she could sit at my desk and do my job nearly as well as I do.

The other female principal spoke in this way about the problems caused by the secretary's few absences:

The work doubles for me . . . . If the nurse is there it's less, but if she isn't . . . then I have to pick up for both of them . . . . I answer the phone . . . take care of attendance . . . give late passes or whatever . . . just fill in where I have to.

The assumption of responsibility for the secretary's work by the female principal was also noted in the comments of the other female principal: "We never discuss 'that's not my job,' [or] 'that's yours' ".

In contrast, male principals speaking about the secretary's absence mentioned the inconvenience it caused them, and how the work would be picked up by others: "It will impact on me because normally she's sitting at that desk and the phone rings and she takes it. That means that other people have to do some covering."

Another male principal commented on his secretary's absence:

[It] puts more pressure back on me, and back on [the clerical aide], and back on the counselor, and things get done, obviously, but I'd rather have her here . . . . I get backed up and I can't do some of the things that I think are more important . . . things that only I can do.

The secretaries to the male principals were also less confident (than their counterparts who worked for female principals) of their boss' ability to carry on without their help. Said one, "They manage . . . . Dick [Mr. John] I think is a little panicky . . . . I think he's thinking 'Oh my gosh, what if something comes up that she ought to be here to take care of it.' "

Another secretary tried to minimize potential problems by remaining available:

If they have questions they'll call me at home . . . . Hopefully everything's spelled out on my desk so that they can handle it . . . . Normally if he's really needing some information right away, like on weekends, he'll go ahead and call me at home and I'll tell him where it's at.

Thus female principals spoke of sharing the burden of extra work, and their secretaries expressed confidence in their principals' ability to do so. Male principals, on the other hand, seemed to rely on others to pick up the slack, and their secretaries were more concerned about the problems their absences might entail.

The tendency of these male principals to differentiate their work from the secretaries' work is also worth noting. In an earlier quote one of the male principals noted how the secretary could "take the load off of him" and thereby allow him to "concentrate on nonroutine decision making and organization." Another male principal, as quoted above, noted how the secretary's absence interfered with his ability to do "more important things." This division of roles among important and less important or routine ones was absent from the female principals' statements. It is perhaps this tendency towards parity in the relationship that helps these female principals to avoid the fear of usurpation of authority expressed by their male colleagues and quoted above.

The female principals also seemed to encourage their secretaries' professional development. Both of these principals spoke of "capitalizing" on their secretaries' skills and of giving them the latitude to use their talents. One female principal related how she had discovered her secretary's talent for writing, a talent she feels she herself lacks: "I wrote something and I said, 'Mary, check it over . . . do it over.' It was beautiful! So I thought, hey, this is something that this lady is really excellent with, and I'm just so pleased."

From that moment on this principal began to give Mary rough drafts, which she wrote in their final form and submitted to the principal for her approval.

The other female principal prefered to do most of her own writing but depended on the secretary "for typing, proofing, and sharing . . . . That if something doesn't sound right don't be afraid to tell me . . . . If you can't understand it then certainly I can't expect 200 parents to understand."

CONCLUSIONS

In spite of the small sample, the differences found in this analysis of the responses of male and female principals, and their respective secretaries, cannot be easily dismissed on the basis of coincidence or particularities. One of the female principals chose her secretary for the job and one would assume that she looked for someone whom she found compatible. The other female principal, however, was hired at the opening of the school year upon the resignation of the school's former principal. She met her secretary on the first day of classes. The interviews were conducted only a few months later, and yet one gets the impression of a long-lasting relationship. All the male principals, on the other hand, had worked with their secretaries for at least 2 years.

In light of these data, it is particularly striking that the secretaries seemed to mirror the responses of their male and female bosses—a tendency that cannot be ascribed to the length of time they have worked together.

Individual differences in the personalities of the secretaries might be called on to explain their responses. But such differences were not readily apparent either in their behavior or in their responses to other questions. As a group, the secretaries were rather consistent in their responses to personal questions about their experience and expectations. The striking differences reported here were only apparent in their responses to questions that touched on their interactions with their principals.

The statements made by principals and secretaries during these interviews fit the interactive model of gender-related behavior proposed by Deaux and Major (1987). They argue that gender is a component of ongoing interactions in which perceivers (in this case principals) emit expectancies, and targets (in this case the school secretaries) negotiate their own identities, all within a particular context. They further argue that gender-linked behavior will be more likely in a perceiver who (a) generally tends towards that behavior, (b) is primed by immediately preceding thoughts and events, (c) is triggered by observable attributes of the target, and (d) is prompted by situations that are sex-linked or that make the target's gender salient.

From the target's perspective, gender-linked behavior will be more likely when (a) the target's self-concept includes that behavior, (b) the target interacts with a perceiver who conveys a particular expectancy to the target, and (c) the situation provides cues that suggest a particular behavior is appropriate.

The situation in the school office appears to be one of those where gender-related issues become salient. The "housekeeping" activities of elementary school secretaries, their affiliation with children, and their tendency to take care of all unassigned tasks are all linked to the mothering role and therefore apt to trigger a person's gender stereotypes. Thus the school office presents a prototypical situation where prototypical behaviors would be predicted (Shutte, Kenrick, & Sadalla, 1985).

In this context the behavior of the two female principals appears more constructive and more likely to lead to a favorable school climate. However, we might speculate on whether the unwillingness of female principals to distance themselves from the secretaries' work, and their unwillingness to absent themselves from the school any more than absolutely necessary, has negative consequences. It may be that male principals who are more inclined to hierarchical relationships and keep one foot in the school and one in the district office are also more likely to be recognized as promotable. Ortiz & Marshall (1988) emphasize the importance of sponsorship to career mobility and also note that sponsors, who are historically males, tend to favor hierarchical control of the organization. Thus educators in this chapter, who view collaboration and cooperation as more suitable to their work, may be overlooked by potential sponsors. In addition, visibility is critical to sponsorship and principals who stay close to their schools are less likely to be identified as promising candidates for promotion.

FIVE

Summary, Conclusions, and Recommendations for Further Research

SUMMARY

When I undertook this study I was interested in documenting the role played by the secretary in the elementary school. For that purpose I decided to observe six secretaries as they worked in their school offices and to conduct interviews with each of the six secretaries and their principals. I also wanted to get a larger view at the national level. This I accomplished through a survey that also allowed me to compare what I learned about the six observed secretaries with a much larger national sample. These data were all congruent. What the secretaries and principals said during the interviews was confirmed through my own observations. The composite of the typical secretary derived from the survey and presented in Chapter 3 was also very similar to the secretaries observed and interviewed. The consistency of the data across these sources suggested reliability.

Two other sources were also investigated: official job descriptions and textbooks used in the preparation of educational administrators. I wanted to compare the views presented in those officially endorsed sources with the views gathered from the school secretaries themselves through the survey, my own observations, and interviews. The data drawn from those official sources were not compatible with the data derived from the survey, observations, and interviews. These findings revealed a school secretary who spent most of her time interacting with people. She thought of herself as an educator and saw a direct relationship between her efficiency in running the school and the success of the school and the children within it.

In contrast, the elementary school secretary described in the official documents resembled a generic business secretary. Job descriptions emphasized the technical skills of the job while slighting the human aspect. And with one exception (Drake & Roe, 1989), the textbooks used in courses designed for the preparation of school administrators, if they mentioned the secretary at all, ignored the public relations responsibilities of the secretary in favor of routine secretarial tasks. The reasons for these differences across data sources will be central to my conclusions later in this chapter and will be followed by recommendations for research and practice.

The data collected for this study have been integrated in the previous chapters, each of which has focused on a topical category rather than on district data sources. In this section I will summarize the data drawn from each of the data sources, giving special attention to the portraits of the elementary school secretaries that emerged at each phase of the study. I will then compare these various portraits and identify similarities and discrepancies among them. This integrated summary description will be compared with the literature in order to ascertain whether this research fits into the framework proposed earlier and whether that proposed framework is useful for understanding the position of the elementary school secretary.

Textbooks of Educational Administration

The most surprising finding in this analysis was the almost total omission of the school secretary from the textbooks examined. However, what is left out of textbooks is as revealing of the author's vision as what is included. It is particularly interesting that several of these authors devote much attention to the school's public relations program. They present models for administrators to follow, they speak of the importance of school-community relations and of attending to the informal networks of communication, and yet they never mention the role of the school secretary in such activities.

The view of the elementary school secretary that can be inferred from most of these textbooks leads readers and students of educational administration to interpret the secretary's position as one that is likely to be useful, perhaps necessary, in performing the clerical routines of the school office, but otherwise tangential and unimportant. Through the omission of the secretary from the texts, aspiring educational administrators could be led to believe that what school secretaries do and how they do it is of little consequence in the schools.

Job Descriptions

The 27 job descriptions analyzed for this study are characterized by their variety. They vary in both format and content. As an aggregate, they display a wide range of duties and responsibilities, all to be carried out by the elementary school secretary. The tasks associated with the duties listed are generally not specified, with the exception of typing speed. The lack of specificity thus suggests that a more precise job definition is likely to take place at each of the schools.

The picture that emerges from these job descriptions is of someone who is charged with a great many responsibilities. The bulk of these are related to office tasks. One would therefore expect these tasks to consume the largest proportion of the school secretary's time.

There is some indication in these job descriptions that those holding these positions may also need to interact with people, and children are sometimes mentioned. Based on these job descriptions, it would seem that the secretaries selected for these positions would be expected to be very adept in their office skills, to have some ability to deal with people, and to be ready to assume responsibility for a great variety of tasks not normally considered as secretarial duties. For example, they may be expected to handle the administration of first aid and the collection of lunch money.

Survey

The data from the survey suggest that elementary school secretaries are responsible for a large variety of tasks. These data also suggest that the secretaries attend to many different clients and that they find it difficult to prioritize them.

Analysis of the survey responses also makes possible a description of the people who hold these positions. They are found to be overwhelmingly female. They usually come to the position later in life when they resume paid employment after their children are in school. Their choice is most often guided by the compatibility between work and family schedules. Survey responses also show that elementary school secretaries earn low salaries, usually about one third of the principal's salary. In spite of the low salary and many responsibilities, they appear to enjoy their jobs.

An unanticipated but welcome part of the survey responses was the wealth of comments offered in response to the two open-ended questions and about the survey itself. These spontaneous comments reveal that this group of women place a high value on education. They see themselves as members of the education team. They derive a great part of their pride from their relationships with the people with whom and for whom they work. They also consider themselves to be efficient secretaries. The abundance of responses also indicates that these secretaries find themselves underpaid and underappreciated. For this state of affairs they tend to blame the school district administrators. With few exceptions, however, they explain that they are not in the job for the money but rather for the personal satisfaction they derive from it.

The portrait that emerges from the survey, then, appears different from that which emerges from the job descriptions. There is nominal similarity in that both show the secretary to be responsible for a wide variety of tasks. However, the respondents to the survey appear to place greater emphasis on the human relationship and educational aspects of their jobs than do the written job descriptions. Survey respondents consistently choose affective terms to describe their positions: "help," "warm," "friendly" and "love" were among the most commonly used words. These secretaries do not seem to neglect the office management part of their jobs. They appear to take great pride in a well-run school and often use the adjective "smooth" to describe their managerial work. But they make a direct connection between their office work and instructional effectiveness.

Judging from the survey responses, the elementary school secretary's position may be described as highly varied; a job demanding a balance between office management skills and skills in dealing with people, particularly children and their parents. The position also appears to attract women seeking paid employment that is compatible with their family responsibilities. Many of these women express and report highly altruistic feelings in their acceptance of low pay, in their pride in the accomplishments of the school or the school children, in their willingness to work overtime without pay, and in their willingness to help others as evidenced by their participation in volunteer organizations.

Interviews

The interview data revealed both large differences and many similarities in the secretary's activities across schools. The interviews were the main avenue for getting the principal's view of the school secretary. Their responses made possible the comparisons between principals and secretaries, secretaries across schools, and principals across schools. The interviews revealed that principals tend to choose their secretaries more for their human relations skills than for their office management skills. Analysis of the interview data also shows that the relationship between principals and their secretaries varies across schools and that it is the principal who defines what the secretary's job is to be. It also appears that the secretaries' presence as the only adult consistently present in the school office results in her assumption of many tasks purely by default. The ambiguity inherent in this situation can be a source of conflict for the secretary.

Data from the interviews also reveal that principals rely on secretaries a great deal for support and for information. For their part, the secretaries appear to be loyal supporters of their principals, even when they are aware of their principal's shortcomings. They also appear willing to adjust their preferences to those of their principals and are uninterested in "running the school." What they most want from their principals, it seems, is support, consideration, and communication.

It became evident during the analysis of these data that the relationship between the principal and the secretary required the pairing of their interviews. Their work could not be understood separately. Each one helped to define the other. The need for this combined interpretation was particularly obvious when the principal's gender was introduced into the analysis. Major differences in the relationships between male and female principals and their secretaries became apparent when this variable was introduced. Male principals tended to personalize the secretaries' representation of the school, used marriage metaphors to describe their relationship, and expressed some concern about possible usurpation of power by their secretaries. Female principals emphasized trust and confidentiality in their relationship with their secretaries, used sports metaphors, and appeared to have established collegial rather than hierarchical relationships in the school office.

School-by-school analysis of the secretary-principal relationship revealed the tendency of secretaries to respond to the principal's definition of the relationship. For example, secretaries working for male principals also used a marriage metaphor, while those working for female principals used sports metaphors. The strong parallel between principal and secretary responses suggests an interactive model of gender behavior (Deaux & Major, 1987).

Observations

Observations revealed that elementary school secretaries not only engage in a variety of tasks but that their days are unpredictable. Observational data indicate that on a given day the secretary may spend the entire day typing; the next day she may never finish typing one letter. There are days when the telephone rings continuously and days when every child in the school appears to be ill, usually when the nurse (or health aide) is not available.

The on-site observations served to confirm the variety of tasks for which the secretary is responsible. These data also showed the unique role of the secretary as the main conduit of information in the school. Only the secretaries communicate on a regular basis with all members of the school staff, including custodial and cafeteria help (if available). They are also the routine receivers and senders of information to the home, and in addition, have almost daily contact with some district personnel. Indeed, the amount and variety of information handled daily by many school secretaries can be staggering. Their position and the variety of sources they routinely tap makes them the information center of the school. As such, the school secretary's position may be perceived as being administratively powerful even in the absence of official responsibilities for administrative decisions.

Integrating the Data

The use of several sources of data in this study provides an opportunity for triangulation across data sources. A high degree of congruence across data sources would favor confidence in the accuracy of the description of elementary school secretaries drawn from these data. Through these summaries I have drawn various portraits of elementary school secretaries. A comparison of these portraits makes three facts evident: (a) There is a high degree of congruence across the data generated from the elementary school secretaries themselves, whether in their survey responses, interviews, or as a result of direct observation; (b) There is also a high degree of congruence between these data and the data gathered through interviews with six elementary school principals; and (c) There is a high degree of discrepancy between the data gathered directly from elementary school secretaries and their principals, and the data extracted through content analysis from official documents.

Quantitative and qualitative analysis of the survey responses result in a description of the elementary school secretary as a person who is engaged in a multiplicity of tasks requiring a wide range of skills. These skills range from secretarial to nursing and include a large measure of human relations skills needed to interact successfully with a large variety of clients. These data also suggest that elementary school secretaries, almost all female and mostly mothers, choose these positions because school schedules mesh conveniently with their family responsibilities. However, they stay in these positions long after their children are grown and independent. Their long tenure in the job is probably related to their enjoyment of the variety inherent in the role. It is also likely that the satisfaction they express about their position is related to the enjoyment they derive from working with children, from helping others, and from the perception that their work contributes to the school's educational goals.

The job is not without its drawbacks, however, and here also there is consistency. Complaints from the respondents to the survey centered primarily on two issues: low salaries and lack of official recognition and, less frequently, on status differences.

The interviews with six elementary school secretaries and their principals confirmed the views expressed by those responding to the survey. These six secretaries all entered the profession in order to successfully combine gainful employment and family responsibilities. All have children but most of their children have passed the dependent stage. They have continued to work because they enjoy the school setting and particularly the opportunity to work with children. As is the case with the secretaries who participated in the survey, these women engage in a great variety of tasks but tend to give higher priority to the human relations rather than to the secretarial aspects of the job. Their principals also favor those priorities and have often chosen them on that basis.

The six principals interviewed also agreed with their secretaries on the centrality of their role. This centrality is evident in their organizational as well as their physical location. Organizationally, these women perform their jobs in the operations center of their schools, the place where records and schedules are kept and resources stored. Their workplace is also the location through which most of the information enters the building, whether through the telephone, correspondence, or through personal visits.

The secretary's organizational location places her at the center of the very active information exchange of the school. Some principals and secretaries used the metaphor "the hub of the wheel" to characterize elementary school secretaries. Their physical location places them at the operational center of the school. They are almost always at that location and are usually the first ones to greet visitors or respond to emergencies. For this reason they are almost always the ones to take care of any unassigned tasks that may develop.

This sometimes includes unofficially assuming administrative responsibilities during the principal's absence.

The principals are very much aware of the many ways in which their secretaries contribute to the efficient operation of their schools and consider their secretaries important members of their staff. They vary in the amount of responsibility they delegate to the secretary, but they are unanimous in valuing the secretary's support and good judgment. This is of particular importance to male principals because they see the secretary as an extension of themselves. Female principals, on the other hand, appear to be particularly aware and appreciative of the secretary's unique access to information that may help them to be better administrators.

Secretaries and principals also agree on the problems and share the concerns expressed by the secretaries who responded to the survey. Low salaries and the lack of district recognition of the secretary's contribution are their major reasons for complaints.

My observations at six school sites confirmed the descriptions rendered above. The centrality of the secretaries, the variety of tasks with which they are routinely charged, and the many other tasks that arise on a daily basis were all evident at the sites. Also evident was the lopsided balance between secretarial and human relations tasks and the secretary's tendency to favor the latter when a choice had to be made.

I found the vital role played by the school secretary in receiving, transmitting, and disseminating information to be the most salient characteristic of the job. She is the only person in the school who, by virtue of location and role, regularly communicates with all members of the school staff, central office personnel, parents, and the community-at-large. She accepts, transmits, and juggles information to and from all of them. She holds the data bank for the school in her head and can usually be counted on to know the names of most students, their parents, all school staff members, district administrators, and often influential members of the community.

Thus the data gathered directly from school secretaries and their principals are highly congruent. Their consistency suggests that the elementary school secretary is an important and valued member of the school staff and a vital link in the communication system within and beyond the school walls.

The data extracted from job descriptions and educational administration textbooks are in stark contrast to other data sources. Activities related to human interaction, particularly with children, are not always mentioned and seldom emphasized. The textbooks of educational administration for the most part either ignore the existence of school secretaries altogether or acknowledge their existence using language similar to the language they may use to describe office equipment.

The weight of the data leaves little doubt that elementary school secretaries play an important role in the school. This is evident from secretaries' responses to the survey, the interviews, and from my own on-site observations. Six elementary principals also agree with that view of the secretary. Why then the neglect and misrepresentation of the position in the official documents? An examination of the literature that served as a framework for this study may help to clarify this discrepancy.

COMPARING THE DATA AND THE LITERATURE

Schools as Organizations

Current theoretical and research-based literature on schools as organizations reviewed in Chapter 2 suggests that schools can be better understood as cultural settings than as business organizations. This is due, at least in part, to the ambiguity inherent in a setting where technologies are unclear, goals ambiguous, and participation fluid. (March & Olsen, 1979).

Schools have also been described as multicultural societies where the goal is to build a common identity that can form the basis for committed action in order to allow the organization to function in concert. (Sergiovanni, 1984). This description is more attuned to the family metaphors used by practitioners to describe schools than to the mechanistic, abstract models that have prevailed until recently in the literature on school administration. (Hanson, 1984)

When schools are seen as cultural settings and when the organizational goal shifts from efficiency to building a common identity, the perception of the secretary's function also changes. In a business setting the secretary's value may lie in her clerical skills first and her human relations skills second. In the school setting the secretary *is* the school for many parents and visitors. If the school is to build a common identity, the secretary's help must be sought, for it is the secretary who is most likely to communicate that identity to the public. The role played by the secretary in representing the school to the public is well understood by the principals interviewed for this study. It is also a responsibility often mentioned by secretaries in their responses to the survey and in the interviews.

The shift in perception also results in a shift in expectations. Principals and secretaries who perceive the school office as just another office in the business model are likely to emphasize the strictly secretarial functions of the job. Those who aim to build a common identity are likely to emphasize the secretary's role in the human interactions that are central to the school.

This is not to suggest that organizational and secretarial skills are not important. The principals and secretaries included in this study emphasized the importance of organizational skills in a setting that is characterized by variety, discontinuity, and unpredictability. But organizational skills in the school setting should be directed at an efficient operation for the purpose of facilitating the school's main function—the delivery of instruction. Many of the secretaries noted in their responses their contribution to the work of teachers and principals and their responsibility for promoting a warm and friendly atmosphere in the school office to facilitate the school's instructional goals. This is in keeping with research on effective schools, which suggests that clerical support may be important to this goal. (See Chapter 2 for this discussion.)

All the secretaries and principals who contributed their views to this study placed their emphasis on the human interactions aspect of the school secretary's job. As has been noted, this view is not reflected in the job descriptions or in the examined textbooks of educational administration. This discrepancy suggests that both of these official views reflect a different perception of the schools and, therefore, of the school secretary's job. The district personnel responsible for developing the job descriptions, and the authors of the textbooks, appear to model the school office after the business office. The secretary, then, is expected to function as any secretary would in that setting.

The Work of Secretaries

The research that discussed secretaries in other settings, reviewed in Chapter 3, suggests that secretarial positions are closely allied with those of their bosses. It is through their bosses that the general skeleton of the job acquires specificity. It is also through them that promotions and other rewards may be achieved. The marriage metaphor is often used in the business setting where the secretary is sometimes called the "office wife." Secretaries in business organizations also appear to be in charge of the emotional life of the organizations, and they are the holders of what Vinnicombe (1980) calls "esoteric organizational knowledge," that is, information about the organization's history and procedures and personal connections established through time. This information can contribute to their bosses' success as managers.

Research on secretaries also points out the difference between various positions defined generically as clerical but extending across a wide range, from pool typist to private secretary. As the secretary moves through the ranks, the boss-secretary relationship also changes. At the lower levels the typist is totally dependent on her boss. At the upper levels the boss' dependence on the secretary is greater. The boss depends on the private secretary for the organizational knowledge she has gained as she has moved through the ranks. These secretaries also tend to control the information flow and to act as surrogates during their bosses' absence. However, even private secretaries are highly dependent on their bosses for establishing the parameters of their jobs and for promotions and other rewards. Their relationship to the boss is based primarily on loyalty and, regardless of their skills, their opportunity for advancing to other positions in the organization is very limited.

Elementary school secretaries resemble private secretaries most closely. They are primarily responsible to one boss who defines the parameters of their job and who is the only one who evaluates them. They are also the repositories of a body of organizational knowledge that is useful and necessary to the principal. Unlike their counterparts in the business world, elementary school secretaries do not move through the organization from the pool typing room to the executive office. They begin at the school office and tend to remain in the same position for long periods of time. The principal moves from school to school, but the secretary is likely to remain at the same school for many years. For the school secretary, organizational knowledge is composed of the history at the school site, knowledge of the community, procedural knowledge, and the information and personal contacts acquired through the years. This body of information is very valuable to principals, particularly those entering a new school setting. It is the equivalent of the "esoteric organizational knowledge" (Vinnicombe, 1980) that corporate secretaries acquire in their settings.

Elementary school secretaries also resemble their business colleagues in the nature of the relationship they establish with their bosses. This relationship appears to be based on loyalty to the boss in both the school and business setting. Marriage and sports metaphors were used by school secretaries and their principals to indicate the importance of balance and compatibility in that relationship.

Principals as well as executives depend on their secretaries for information and in both situations the secretaries often act as surrogates during their bosses' absence. This places the secretary in an ambiguous position. Most of the time she is expected to follow orders, but at any given moment she may be in charge and expected to make decisions. This creates a situation of what I call intermittent power, which may be presumed to make large demands on a secretary's emotional resources. Navigating these treacherous waters requires exquisite sensitivity to time and place in order to avoid upsetting the balance of power and threatening the administrator.

A major difference between elementary school secretaries and their business colleagues is in their sphere of responsibility. Private secretaries in business operate within a limited sphere. Although the work necessitates contact with many others within and outside the organization the secretary is responsible to only one boss and needs to answer to only one set of demands. Conflicts may arise, but they are likely to be conflicts between loyalty to the boss and loyalty to an abstract organization. Research (Kanter, 1977; Vinnicombe, 1980) indicates that secretaries in the business setting tend to give priority to their bosses to whom they give their personal loyalty.

Elementary school secretaries occupy a much more ambiguous position. Although the principal is their only official boss, the school secretary has responsibility to many others as well—teachers, parents, support staff, and particularly to the students. Conflicts that arise in the school setting are more likely to test the secretary's allegiance to members of these various groups and trap her in the middle. Business secretaries can easily identify the person to whom they are responsible. School secretaries have difficulty separating their various client groups. When asked to whom they owe their primary responsibility, they prefer to answer with a listing of their client groups. They see themselves as responsible to all of them. When forced to limit their response to just one client type, it is not the principal but the students to whom they say they are primarily responsible. This difference in the range of responsibility requires the elementary school secretary to continually juggle the demands of her clients not only at the level of service, but sometimes in situations with moral or ethical implications. This situation makes the school setting not only more demanding than the business setting, but also a setting with far greater potential for conflict.

Women and Work

The review of gender-related research reported in Chapter 2 provides two perspectives for analyzing the elementary school secretary's position. On the one hand, findings from this research suggest that the position of women in the organizational structure limits their opportunity for advancement to more challenging positions. According to that research, a structural limitation influences women's aspirations to more challenging jobs. The lack of opportunity results in women seeking their rewards within the social aspects of the job (Kanter, 1978). Another view suggests that the differential psychosocial development of males and females results in gender differences that affect adult behavior. According to this line of research, women's development centers on the elaboration of intimacy, relationships, and care while men's development is more likely to result in an emphasis on autonomy and responsibility (Gilligan, 1982).

Data from this study suggest that elementary school secretaries derive their greatest satisfaction in the job from their work relationships and, further, that a strong altruistic strain underlies these relationship. The emphasis appears to be in helping others. This interest in helping is also apparent in the reported high rate of participation in volunteer organizations and activities. It is also expressed in the secretaries' statements about salary and recognition. School secretaries are sadly aware of their low salaries and lack of official recognition, but many point out that they find their satisfaction elsewhere. Their satisfaction, they say, comes from helping others and from contributing to the educational endeavor. These elementary school secretaries also take pride in their competence and efficiency, but when they do so it is usually in relation to their contribution to education rather than as an abstract accomplishment.

Previous research on school secretaries, cited in Chapter 3, corroborates these findings. It also suggests that these women, as a group, tend to downplay monetary rewards and emphasize relationships. That research (Simon, 1972) also found that principals, teachers, and secretaries hold different expectations for the school secretary and highlights the potential for conflict inherent in these differences. As was noted before, this is one of the characteristics that distinguish school secretaries from their colleagues in the business world.

The three perspectives adopted in Chapter 2 as an organizational framework for conducting the literature review help to illuminate the position of the elementary school secretary. They provide a framework within which the elementary school secretary, a female clerical worker operating in a school setting, can be understood. Through the integration of these three perspectives, similarities between school secretaries and secretaries in other settings become readily apparent. Also apparent are the peculiarities of the school setting, which contribute another set of demands that affect school secretaries in important ways.

Data from this study seem to confirm the view that females derive their rewards as adults form their personal relationships. It could also be argued that the structural limitations imposed on the school secretary's position, that is, minimal opportunities for advancement, force these women to turn their attention to their work relationships as their source of satisfaction. But this latter argument is weakened by the evidence provided in the survey that show these women to be active participants in many volunteer activities. Findings from earlier research on school secretaries also tend to corroborate the findings presented here.

The school mother

The do-it-all, be-everything-to-all perception of the elementary school secretary that emerges from the data and the observations also adds another dimension to the marriage metaphor. While the secretary in the business office tends to become the "office wife," the secretary in the school office becomes the "school mother." This metaphor was in fact used by one respondent to the survey in explaining what gave her pride in her job.

> I am referred to as the heart of the school, the mother. I help to make everything run smoothly and I give so many a feeling of security and confidence with my presence. When I am absent everyone waits for my return to help with problems and set them in the right direction.

It is also implicit in descriptions of the school secretary as the person who is "always there," the one who takes over in any emergency, or, as one teacher commented, "the lifeline of the school."

Elementary school secretaries, as I have shown, have much in common with other clerical workers, especially with private secretaries. However, they perform their work in the elementary schools, a particular type of workplace. The uniqueness of the setting would be expected to have implications for their role. Schools are, of course, public rather than private places that serve a multilayered clientele but are primarily child-centered and populated largely by females. In addition, the administrator in the school office is more likely to be male while the secretary is almost invariably female.

The secretary in the school office is besieged by continuous demands that tend to be unpredictable and overlapping. Unlike the business secretary, the school secretary spends a large part of the day in direct or telephone contact with people, most of them from her client groups.

All of these characteristics of the school and school office place special demands on the women who hold the secretarial positions. They often cite the need for flexibility in the job and they note the importance of calm and patience in dealing with upset parents, teachers, or children. They also see their position primarily as one designed to help, particularly to help children. And they spend a good portion of their time ensuring the safety of the students whether through application of first aid or by refusing an unauthorized request to remove a child from the school. It is not surprising then that several of them refer to themselves as the "mother" or the "heart" of the school.

Mothers, like secretaries, are expected to be all things to all people. They are also expected to take care of the housekeeping aspects of the home. They are the ones who remember birthdays and plan celebrations, and they assume much of the responsibility for the daily safety of those under their care.

Private business secretaries are often called the "office wives." They take care of their (usually) male bosses who rely on them to buffer demands and keep them on track. Some of this behavior, according to Kanter (1977), may be due to the dependent relationship between boss and secretary. In business offices, the secretaries at the upper end of the hierarchy move with their boss and depend on the boss for their evaluation as well as for career advancement. This relationship, according to Kanter, encourages fealty.

The elementary school secretary is also dependent on the principal for her evaluation, and she establishes a loyal relationship to the individual occupying that position. This relationship appears to be less exclusive, however. Unlike her business counterpart, she tends to divide her priorities between the principal and the students. Her career advancement does not depend on the principal. In fact, there are few possibilities for any type of advancement.

While principals come and go, she remains at a school for many years and becomes attached to a clientele that is much broader than that of a business secretary. Her responsibilities to the boss must always be balanced against her responsibilities to students, teachers, and parents. She becomes a part of the school community. I am reminded of a marriage after the children are born, when the loyalty that existed between spouses is challenged by the need to protect and attend to the children.

All but one of the elementary school secretaries interviewed stated unequivocally that their first responsibility was to the children. And those responding to the survey ranked children, as well as the school administrator, as their number one priority. The school secretaries had difficulty choosing among their various roles. Their predicament is well described by Lobsenz & Blackburn (1968): "Should she, if indeed she can, distribute her physical and psychic energies equally among her roles? What if she prefers one to the relative exclusion of others?" (p. 115). These authors go on to note the extraordinary energy and courage that is required to face these conflicts. But although their words are highly appropriate in this context, their topic is not school secretaries; it is wives and mothers.

In their responses to the question of what makes them proud, elementary school secretaries also indicated an unbusinesslike tendency to associate love and help with their work—responses that sound more like those of a mother than a secretary.

Perhaps most indicative of the elementary school secretary's role as the school mother were the expectations expressed by the principals and by the secretaries themselves: to be "always there," and to assume any responsibility whenever necessary. These expectations are more closely allied to mothers than to office workers.

There is yet another interesting aspect to the secretary as "school mother." As noted in Chapter 1, increasing demands for clerical support in the schools coincided with increased bureaucratization of the institution. Teacher-principals evolved into managers and expert administrators. It may be argued that school managers, following the business model, would demand clerical help. Alternatively, and taking into consideration the coincidental decline in the proportion of female school administrators during this period, we may argue that as the school became more businesslike, a previously provided nurturing role was left vacant. This role, traditionally handled by females, was filled by the school secretary: the school mother.

CONCLUSIONS

The research reported here was undertaken with the purpose of arriving at a description of elementary school secretaries. It is meant to fill a void in the literature and to contribute to a better understanding of the school as an organization. Findings from this research provide a description of the women who fill these positions, their personal characteristics, expressed perceptions, values, and concerns, as well as the characteristics of their work.

The remarks that follow are tempered by the knowledge that the secretaries studied for this project constitute a select group. Those participating in the survey were all members of their professional association and were therefore perhaps more committed and dedicated than their colleagues. The secretaries and principals observed and interviewed were selected by their supervisors as "good" examples. There are no "bad" examples here. There is also very limited representation here from schools in large urban areas where the pressures may multiply and greatly affect the conduct of the role. Nonetheless, the congruence of the findings reported suggests that the concluding remarks that follow are justified.

Analysis of the data gathered for this study tend to confirm the popular view of elementary school secretaries as multitalented individuals who serve many different clients and who play a central role in the operation of the school. This is the view that is presented in the media and expressed by school practitioners, but it is different from the view of elementary school secretaries that can be gleaned from official job descriptions and from educational administration textbooks.

The discrepancy in these views appears to be due, at least in part, to traditional views of schools as organizations patterned after the business model. In such a setting the school office would operate much like any other office, and the secretary's job would be mainly concerned with clerical and secretarial tasks. It is questionable whether such a perception of the secretary's role is accurate even for the business setting. It is certainly not accurate for the school setting. The data reported here provide strong evidence of the predominance of human interaction in the school setting. This emphasis on human interaction in the school office is congruent with the recent theoretical construct discussed in Chapter 2 of the school as a cultural setting.

Another contributing factor to the discrepancy between the official views and the view of the secretaries that emerged from the analysis offered here is the gender of elementary school secretaries. Gender characteristics of the work force have been known to influence the perceptions held about the position: "We find that gender contributes to the social definition of skill—a minority of jobs, it would seem, are defined as being in the lowest clerical grade, not because of the technical content of the work itself, but because the job is usually carried out by a woman." (Compton & Jones, 1984, p. 4). It appears that the job of the elementary school secretary belongs in that group.

The discrepancy between the officially promulgated perception and the data-based description reported here would be tolerable except for the way it affects the rewards that accrue to the women who perform these jobs. The low salaries that secretaries receive are not commensurate with the work they perform or with the responsibilities they assume. Even less appropriate is the lack of recognition of the contribution elementary school secretaries make to the operation of the school. This lack of recognition is evident, not only in the official views described in earlier chapters, but also in the research that has been conducted in the schools. It seems to be a result of what Lofland (1975) calls "the thereness of women" who, like the servants in the mystery stories, are always present but remain merely part of the scene. Research on school principals and on school effectiveness have apparently been affected by this syndrome.

There is yet another possible explanation for the discrepancy between the official and data-based views of the elementary school secretary. It may be that official perceptions are not misguided, only conveniently assumed for the sake of financial advantages. It is evident from the data reported here that elementary school secretaries are committed to their jobs and that they derive a great deal of satisfaction from their ability to help others and to contribute to education. They are champions of the educational process and they are caring people.

There are those who might take issue with women who take jobs that place them in the positions described here. I am not among them. I believe that there are jobs in society that require care, nurturance, and many other qualities that are often bestowed on women through socialization. There is nothing wrong with those jobs or with the women who prefer them. There is, however, something definitely wrong with a society that offers better rewards to those who work with "things" than to those who work with people, particularly children. The problem, as I see it, is one of exploitation of those women who take difficult, demanding jobs that are essential to the society's well-being, and yet are not properly rewarded for that effort.

Since elementary school secretaries as a group demonstrate these so-called "feminine" characteristics, decision makers might consider financial rewards unnecessary and fear that recognition of any sort might just lead to increased demands. This is not a pleasant conclusion to entertain, but it needs to be considered. It does appear that financial rewards are not a strong motivating factor for these women; therefore, why spend the money? This is, of course, not much different than the salaries and conditions experienced by helping professionals. As in those cases, however, the question is not one of finances but of ethics. It is ethical for any institution, but most particularly for one charged with the education of children, to disregard or ignore the skills, loyalty, and commitment of their employees for the sake of financial gains? A society that condones such actions cannot be called fair and just. It risks mass disaffection and alienation. However, the assumption that school administrators may be taking advantage of the good will of the women who hold these positions may be totally unfounded. It is preferable to assume that the lack of recognition previously noted is only due to a lack of understanding. In that case the findings reported here ought to make a difference.

RECOMMENDATIONS

For Policy Makers

The findings reported here suggest that elementary school secretaries can be an important asset in the achievement of the school's goals. Current policies tend to impede rather than advance that possibility, however. The recommendations that follow are meant to suggest a few ways in which the secretary's contribution might be better realized.

1. Enhance job descriptions of elementary school secretaries to make them more compatible with the reality of the job.

2. Enhance job descriptions to require different qualifications for entry into the job. Most important would be increased attention to interpersonal skills, willingness to tolerate the unpredictability and variety of the job, evidence of good judgment, and interest in children and education.

3. Provide opportunities for professional training, specifically in the areas indicated by the school secretaries who responded to the survey: child development and cross-cultural understanding.

4. Consult with school secretaries in the development of district and school policies and in the preparation for their implementation. Their aggregated experience and knowledge of the school office can lead to more efficient and effective functioning.

5. Consider the secretary a contributor to the school's instructional goals. Include her in the planning and keep her informed of new developments. Whether well informed or not, secretaries will play a part in communicating the goals of the school to the public. Make sure her communication is accurate and beneficial.

6. In a joint effort with the faculty and secretary, negotiate clear guidelines for the secretary's job and see that they are followed.

7. Consider the special talents of the school secretary and ensure they are used to advantage in the school office.

8. Protect the secretary from being exploited (i.e. baby-sitting detail). They are usually willing to pitch in when necessary but continuous abuse of such kindness requires the intervention of the principal.

9. Find ways to provide health services to the children through qualified professionals. This may currently be a dangerous responsibility for school secretaries and one they do not relish. It is no longer a case of sniffles and broken bones. Many children with serious

physical disabilities are now in attendance at the local school, and the burden continues to fall on the secretary.

10. Above all, give due recognition to the secretary's role in the elementary school and reward her appropriately.

For Further Research

The research reported here is the first attempt at a comprehensive description of elementary school secretaries. Therefore it raises as many questions as it answers. Some of those questions constitute interesting avenues for further research. Answers to the research questions suggested below would contribute not only to a better understanding of the school secretary's position but also to a clearer understanding of schools as organizations.

1. How is the role of the school secretary affected by:
   • the age of the student population
   • the size of the school and/or district
   • the ethnic and socioeconomic composition of the student body
2. How do the roles of school secretaries and principals interface with each other, and how do the people occupying those roles contribute to each other's effectiveness?
3. What is the relationship between the school secretary's role and the school's perceived effectiveness?
4. Is the effect of the principal's gender on his or her relationship with the school secretary also apparent in other settings?
5. What are the variables that contribute to a successful work relationship between the principal and the secretary?
6. What alternative organizational structures can be devised in the schools in order to make better use of the skills of principals and secretaries? For example, would it be useful to pair a principal as instructional leader and a secretary as administrative assistant to manage a school?
7. Is the altruism characteristic of elementary school secretaries a function of self-selection or does it evolve in the job?
8. What is the best academic and experiential preparation for the school secretary's job?
9. What type of professional development do school secretaries require?
10. What role can the school secretaries play in school improvement programs?

These are some of the questions that should be answered if the role of the school secretary is to be adequately recognized in the operation of schools. It is particularly important that the centrality of her role be taken into account in the current concern for school improvement and the role of the principal.

This report began with a young student asking a school secretary, "Are you the office?" It now ends with the answer, "Yes, the school secretary *is* the office." Who she is and what she does in that office cannot be ignored by those who are concerned about schools.

Research Methods

Three different types of data were gathered for this study: qualitative data, quantitative data, and archival data. Each of these types of data required a different method of data collection. Qualitative data were gathered through on-site observations and interviews, quantitative data were derived from the results of a national survey, and archival data were obtained from job descriptions and textbooks of educational administration.

QUALITATIVE DATA

Two methods were used to gather qualitative data for this study: site observations and interviews. Both types of data were gathered at each of six schools in two different school districts. The districts are located in small cities close to a large metropolitan area in the southwestern United States.

Selection of School Sites

Selection of the sites was guided by a number of limiting factors. A geographical limitation was imposed first. All districts considered were within the boundaries of a large city in the southwest, and all the sites were elementary schools.

The perceived quality of the principal-secretary relationship, the length of time they had been working together, the gender of the principal (all secretaries in the area are female), and the willingness of both principal and secretary to participate in the research study were additional limiting factors.

The first of these, the perceived quality of the principal-secretary relationship, was imposed in order to limit the sites to those where a "good"relationship was believed to exist. The lack of previous descriptive data on elementary school secretaries made it imperative that conflict situations be avoided. The purpose of the study is to describe the normal situation of the elementary school secretary, not to identify conflictive situations. For the judgment of what constituted "good" situations, the researcher relied on the judgment of district personnel.

The length of time the principal and secretary had been working together was also considered. An effort was made to find sites that represented different points in a continuum of length of experience working together. The six pairs of principals and secretaries represented a range from 5 months to 5 years of time working together.

The original plan had been to limit the sample to four schools in one district. Later, when the first phase of observations suggested that gender might have an influence on the principal-secretary relationship, two additional schools in another district were added. This permitted the inclusion of another female elementary school principal. A second school in the same district, but with a male principal, was also included in order to facilitate within district comparisons.

Last, the willingness of district officials to allow the researcher access to the schools, and of principals and secretaries to agree to participate, further limited the choices. Two districts contacted denied the request outright. The final selection included two districts and six schools that varied in size from 244 to 818 students. Their student populations varied by ethnicity and socioeconomic class. Four of the administrators were male and two were female; the length of time the principal and the secretary had been working together ranged from a few months to more than 5 years.

The brief descriptions of the districts and schools that appear in the text are expanded and elaborated in the pages that follow. Inevitably this results in some redundancy but also provides a deeper level of detail for interested readers.

District 1

At the time of the study, the total student population in District 1 was 7,000 students of which almost 4,000 attended the seven elementary schools. It was a growing district in an area that was quickly changing from rural to industrial. Four of the schools included in the study were in District 1: Washington, Dewey, Fillmore, and Grant.

Washington School

Washington School was located about as distant from the center of District 1 as possible. The area around the school remained rural, although the district's economic structure was rapidly changing from rural to industrial. The school building was only 1 year old; in fact, it was not yet completed.

The ethnic make up of the student population was 75% white, 23% Mexican American, and 2% American Indian. A 52% mobility ratio suggests this was not an altogether stable area.[1]

There were 11 teachers and more than 250 students at Washington School. Three itinerant teachers, 4 special teachers (e.g., special education, band counselor) and 6.5 support staff, including the secretary and attendance clerk, completed the staff.

The school office space was rather cramped because it was designed as a classroom. There would not be an office proper until the rest of the school was completed, and that was not expected to happen until population increases placed demands on the existing space.

The small office at Washington School (see Figure 2.2) was divided by a high counter where supplies were stored. A seating/waiting area faced the counter. The secretary and attendance clerk's desks were on the other side of the counter next to each other. Each one had a typewriter, but they shared a telephone. There were three offices behind them: the principal's medium-sized office, a very small office shared by various support staff, and a medium-sized space where some copying equipment, teachers' supplies, a water cooler, and a coffee pot were kept. Teachers congregated there before and after classes and during their breaks. The teachers' mailboxes were also nearby.

The nurse's office was at the end of this office complex; a washroom was across from it. Filing cabinets filled much of the remaining available space leaving only one-person-wide alleyways between work areas.

The office walls were almost totally covered. The largest wall near the principal's office was completely covered by a large outline map of the United States. Stars within each state represented staff and student states of origin. The wall behind the secretary and attendance clerk served to display certificates, greeting cards, and cartoons. Several of the certificates honored Diane Green, the school secretary, as "outstanding." A cartoon representing the multiple demands to which she must answer (a gift from the art teacher at the school where she began as an office aide) was prominently featured. All of these mementoes were attractively framed and aesthetically combined on the wall.

The wall behind the seating/waiting area, outside the counter, bore then-current displays of newspaper clippings about the school or school district, photographs of new entrants to the school and, for a while, baby pictures of the whole staff. Above it, the school's logo, "The Cowhands" was displayed. The displays on the wall were changed frequently by the secretary. They were always colorful and artistically displayed.

Ms. George, the principal of Washington School, lived in a suburban area about 20 miles away. Diane lived within the district but not in the school's neighborhood. The attendance clerk lived next door to the school. Diane Green was a tall, slender, soft-spoken woman whose continuous eye contact as she listened suggested undivided attention. She smiled often and dressed simply and neatly but comfortably. Her movements were always fluid, never abrupt, giving an appearance of calm even when she was very busy.

Dewey School

During most of the observation period the situation at Dewey School was unusual. District 1 had experienced some problems with the installation of an air conditioning system at several schools. As a result the construction work was just getting started at the end rather than at the beginning of the summer as had been planned. Several schools had to be closed until at least the bulk of the work was completed. Through the cooperation of area churches, entire school populations were moved to church meeting halls and school was resumed on time.

Dewey School was one of these schools. It also required the most extensive air conditioning work among all the district schools, so their stay at the temporary site was the longest. The total group of students, teachers, support and administrative staff was moved to a large, modern, and handsome church meeting hall. It was as good a situation as could be hoped for, but it was not the school. Adjustments had to be made by everyone. For the purposes of this study, the effects of this temporary situation on the clerical/administrative work of the school was most important.

The temporary site (see Figure 2.3) was built roughly as a rectangle within a rectangle. The outer rectangle had small classrooms and a few offices all the way around. The inner rectangle was a very large open area. The primary level students were located in this open area in classroom-sized groups. Portable chalkboards and a few materials were assigned to each group. The children sat on the floor and wrote on lap boards. The noise level was extremely high.

The older students were assigned to the classrooms along the outer rectangle. The rooms were too small for the groups and the chairs were of the light, folding variety. They also needed to use lap boards because the chairs were armless.

There were two executive-type offices available (a few rooms were locked and unavailable). One of these was used by the counselor; the other one was shared by the principal and the secretary. This office was next to a boardroom where teachers ate their lunch. A few smaller offices along the outer rectangle were used by itinerant teachers. Since there were no mailboxes for the teachers, all communications had to be hand delivered.

For a while Mr. John, the principal, attempted to keep the office at the school site opened for new registrants and to take care of telephone calls. However, frequent power interruptions at the school made this idea impractical, and soon the secretary, Edna Brown, was moved to the church site.

At the church the secretary did not have a desk or files to rely on. Questions often had to wait until someone went over to the school about five miles away to get the information. There was no copier, and for a while not even a typewriter. Copying work had to be taken to the district office about 10 miles away. The typewriter was brought later, enabling the secretary to do some work at the church. Only a few supplies were brought along; the rest had to be fetched from the school. Often the errand runner was unfamiliar with the requests and would return with the wrong material, forms, or records.

There were three telephones, all on separate lines. One telephone was located in the counselor's office, one in the principal's office, and one in the hall near the main entrance. The one in the hall was a wall phone, set high enough on the wall so that it was not comfortable to sit while using it. The room directly beside it was used as the nurse's office.

The main entrance was wide and spacious. Comfortable upholstered chairs were set against the sides. Religious pictures and photographs of leading church members were on the wall. A folding table was placed against the far wall. This was where the school office staff set up "the office." Someone was usually sitting there acting as receptionist. Most often it was the attendance clerk, but others, including myself, sometimes performed the same function.

Few of the standard pieces of office equipment were available: an electric pencil sharpener, a few paper clips, some writing implements, and the forms required for registration. All the equipment and materials used by the school during the week had to be removed from the site every Friday, so there was little incentive to bring in any more than was absolutely necessary.

The student population of Dewey School was 440; 55% of these were minority students, mostly Mexican American. The school was located in a low-income area. Normally most of the children walked to school, but they were bused to the church. Edna Brown, the secretary, and Mr. John, the principal at Dewey School, lived in nearby towns. The attendance clerk lived in the neighborhood.

Edna was on the short and plump side although not fat. She dressed smartly, always wore heels, and kept her hair neatly coiffed. She had large expressive eyes and smiled often and easily.

Fillmore School

Fillmore School was the largest school included in the sample. The student population was 818, including four sections of special education. Students classified as white comprised 57% of the school population; the next largest group was Mexican Americans at 35%. African Americans, American Indians, Orientals, and others made up the difference. The population at Fillmore was made up of moderately mobile students (45%) from the low socioeconomic levels. Half of them received free lunch, but the absentee rate was low (4%).

The staff was large, consisting of 31 classroom teachers, 10 special program teachers and 22 others as support staff. Mr. Millard, the principal, lived in the district, while the attendance clerk and Kathy Orange, the secretary, lived in the neighborhood of the school.

The school building was large, open, modern, and only five years old. The school office was also spacious and open (see Figure 2.4). A low counter separated the visitors' waiting area from the office proper, which was furnished in simple institutional style.

The nurse's office and a small infirmary were to the right immediately upon entering the office. The secretary and attendance clerk's desks were to the left behind the counter; another counter of the same height marked the boundary between the office and the passageway to the principal's office in the rear. If one continued to walk beyond the principal's office, the supply room would be to the right and beyond that, behind the principal's office, was the counselor's office. At the end of that hall were the teachers' lounge and lunch area. Farther on but connected to the lounge/lunch area was the staff workroom.

Within the office proper and between the two desks sat the intercom. Behind the attendance clerk's desk the teachers' mailboxes were positioned in such a way that teachers could reach them easily through a door leading from the hall almost directly to the principal's office.

The office was sparsely decorated. Several western landscapes hung along the longer wall. On the wall near the secretary the school's logo was displayed and also pencils and t-shirts with the school name and/or logo, which were available for sale through the PTO. The other materials attached to the wall were all utilitarian: schedules, calendars, the month's menu, and assorted school notices.

Thirty-two-year-old Kathy Orange, the secretary at Fillmore, was the youngest of the six secretaries observed. Of average height and weight, she dressed neatly (sewed most of her own clothes) but conservatively, smiled often, moved quickly, and was particularly adept at handling many things at once—a talent that was useful in her busy office.

Grant School

Grant School was one of the larger schools where observations took place. The student population of 707 students was composed of 60% white and 34% Mexican Americans. African Americans and American Indians made up the balance. The population was mostly from the lower-middle class; almost one-half (48%) of the students received free lunch. The population was also highly mobile (83%), and the absentee rate was high (16%).

The staff at Grant School was composed of 29.5 classroom teachers, 6 teachers assigned to special programs, and 12 additional support staff. Elsie Lavender, the secretary, and Mr. Ulysses, the principal, lived in the district. The attendance clerk grew up in and still lived in the neighborhood.

The office at Grant School was quite small (see Figure 2.5). There was barely enough room for the secretary and attendance clerk's desks. On the left, as one entered the office, there was a five-foot-high counter. Across from it were the nurse's office and a small infirmary. The attendance clerk's desk was right behind the counter. She sat facing the secretary whose desk was on the other side of a narrow passageway that led to the photocopier. Directly behind the secretary was a small table with a pencil sharpener and stacks of materials that varied depending on the day. To the left of the secretary was the typewriter. When typing, the secretary faced a passageway that led from the outside door directly to the principal's office in the rear. A right turn in front of this door led down a narrow hall to a storage room and bathroom on the left, and to the counselor's office on the right. At the end of this hall was a large work and storage area; to the left was the faculty lounge. The teachers' mailboxes were located in the large work area that could be reached through the main office or through a door leading to another building.

The main office at Grant School had few decorations. Thematic, commercially produced cutouts were placed around the bulletin boards. Sometimes selected children's work was displayed, but the bulletin boards were usually covered with schedules and notices, all in "ditto purple."

Elsie Lavender, the secretary, was in her mid-forties and very slender. She was witty, sometimes cutting, in her remarks that were laced with folk expressions. She usually dressed smartly and almost always wore high heels.

District 2

The total student population in District 2 was more than 13,000, of which almost 11,000 attended the 22 elementary schools. This district was dominated by a state university, and many of the parents of the students were associated with the university. Two of the schools included in this study were in this district: Hayes and Alvarez Schools.

Hayes School

Hayes School was a small school with 244 students and 11 classroom teachers. It was located near a university in a stable neighborhood. The mobility rate was only 25%.

The racial and ethnic composition of the student body was 66% white, 15% black and 15% Mexican American. Three percent of the students were classified as American Indian and 1% as Oriental. This was the first year at this school for Mr. Rutherford, the principal, and Sandy Pink, the secretary. They had worked together for two years at a larger school. The principal was appointed to this smaller school so that he could devote some of his time to the administration of the district's summer school and to the development of an after-school program for the district. The secretary was transferred with him because of her expertise with the summer school program and because the former secretary at Hayes was unwilling to take on this added responsibility.

The 15-year-old building was much larger than was required for the number of students attending. Whole wings were given over to district offices. It was not a particularly attractive building—box-like and plain—but it was adjacent to a park. Both the park and the building grounds were attractively kept.

The main office (see Figure 2.6) was not very large, but it was uncrowded. Visitors entered a waiting area which ended at a tall counter. The office proper was behind the counter. The principal's office was to the left as one walked toward the secretary. She sat facing the entrance. Her desk was placed off-center so that the counter did not obstruct her vision of the main door. To the left of the secretary was the intercom and then a storage room. A computer was also set up there. To the right of the secretary was an ample nurse's office and infirmary area. Another computer was set up directly behind the secretary. This one was connected to a district computer and was used only for recording attendance.

The walls around the office were covered with attractive, sometimes "cute," commercially produced posters with inspirational sayings on them. Most of these sayings expressed affection and/or encouragement.

Sandy Pink was in her late thirties, slim, and always attractively dressed. She gave the appearance of being in motion all the time, even when she was standing still. She smiled frequently and always had cheerful words for people who passed by her desk.

Alvarez School

Alvarez School had the distinction of having been named after a retired district custodian and his wife, a food service worker. Mr. Alvarez and his family attended schoolwide activities regularly. A large photograph of the honored couple was prominently displayed at the entrance of the school. Also prominently displayed were cabinets holding many trophies won by students and/or faculty at Alvarez. The school's logo, large and colorful, was displayed here also.

The Alvarez School building was almost 10 years old but had been well maintained and appeared newer than that. It was a modern design, built around a central library/media center.

The school office (see Figure 2.7) was located to the right of the main entrance and along a central corridor leading in one direction to the cafeteria, and to the library in the other. Support staff offices were located to one side of this corridor. Next to them was a kindergarten. The corridor was very wide and also served as a waiting area for children coming to receive special services, for visitors, or sometimes as a place where volunteers could help with some clerical work. Two tables and several chairs were available for these uses.

There was no door or wall separating the main office area from the corridor—only a low counter. The secretary's desk sat against the far wall in that area. She faced the corridor when she typed. The intercom was in the corner along with the district computer used for recording attendance. At the other end of the counter, another computer and its printer were set up. This one was protected by a plastic cover suggesting less than daily use. The principal's office was across from the secretary. In the back, between both office areas, was the nurse's office and a small infirmary.

The teachers' mailboxes were located near the secretary's desk, while their workroom and lounge areas were on the other side of the main entrance. A photocopier, other duplicating equipment, and another computer were also located there.

Ms. Alonso, the principal, was assigned to Alvarez School upon the unexpected resignation of her predecessor. The opening day of the school year was also her first day as the principal.

The secretary, Mary Lime, was in her late forties, dressed neatly and conservatively, wore "sensible" shoes, and was slightly overweight. She had the appearance of a kindly, youthful grandmother. Her demeanor was always gentle and calm.

These six schools were the setting for the case studies conducted for this research. They differed in size and complexity, in student population served, and in the length of the principal-secretary work relationship. They resembled each other in that they were all recommended by their respective school districts as "good" school offices, where the secretary and the principal worked well together.

Access

The first contact with District 1 was made in early August 1984. The study was explained to a district supervisor who acted as liaison between myself and the school sites. Inclusion of female as well as male principals, if possible, was also requested. District 1 had only one female principal (at Washington School) and she agreed to participate. Another early participant was Dewey School; Fillmore and Grant Schools were contacted a few weeks later. Those three schools had male principals. Schools in District 2 were not contacted until November.

Similar approaches were used in both districts. Principals were first called by the Central Office (CO) supervisor acting as liaison. That call was followed by a call from me and a request for an appointment to discuss the project. They also received explicit commitment that their school would not be used unless they agreed to participate. They could decide whether or not to participate after the project and its requisites and demands on them were fully explained.

Initial meetings varied from school to school. At one school the researcher and the principal spoke only briefly and informally. He had told the Central Office contact that he would grant permission to proceed with observations for the study, but he failed to notify the secretary, who was quite surprised to learn of the study. This pattern was repeated at two other schools, that is, the principal knew and had given at least preliminary agreement, but the secretaries were not informed until after the researcher arrived. At the other three schools the secretary had been consulted and was expecting the researcher. At two of these schools, both in District 2, the principal, the researcher, and the secretary sat down together to discuss the project and exchange questions. At one of these schools this meeting was continually interrupted by children looking for the nurse who was absent that day. The principal and the secretary took turns attending to the children; sometimes it took both women to take care of the situation. After these preliminary meetings, secretaries and principals in all six schools agreed to participate in the study.

Site Observations

Observations in the six elementary school offices were conducted for a total of 180 hours over a 6-month period. A schedule was followed to ensure that observations in each school took place at different hours throughout the day. Handwritten notes and audio tapes were used to record the data.

The purpose of the observations was to provide a first-hand account of the elementary school secretary's work in the school office. The use of this research technique was particularly appropriate for studying the school secretary for whom a descriptive literature does not yet exist.

Observations were conducted for 2-hour periods at different times during the day. The first pair of schools, Dewey and Washington, were observed for a longer period of time than the other four and the second pair for a longer period than the last pair. The observer sat by the secretary, off to the side away from the traffic, during most of the observations. This was more easily accomplished in some schools than others. Office space was very limited at Washington and Grants Schools. At Dewey School, temporary facilities also made observation difficult. There were times when the observer became a participant because someone asked for help directly, as was the case when a Spanish-speaking family needed an interpreter, or because circumstances required intervention, as in situations where many things were happening at once. In addition, principals and secretaries often made comments to the researcher and sometimes asked for her opinion on issues that arose during the observation.

Continuous audio-taping during the two-hour period was supplemented with handwritten notes by the researcher. Staff and parents visiting the school were usually curious about the stranger sitting by the secretary taking notes and with a microphone clipped on her clothing. The secretaries spontaneously and universally introduced the researcher as "my shadow" although that term had not been used during the introductory meetings. The explanation offered to inquires about the purpose of the study usually elicited positive comments about the secretary such as: "about time" and "secretaries run the schools." In one case a volunteer parent called it an evaluation. When corrected, she insisted that was the hidden purpose. Fortunately, the secretary did not appear to feel threatened by that possibility.

Analysis

Notes and audio tapes were integrated in one of two ways. Interactions were arranged in charts with five columns. They were labeled: time, who, what, outcome, and comments. The first two columns corresponded to information about who was involved and the direction of the involvement, e.g., "secretary gives information about new entrant to principal." In the next column the outcome of the interaction, e.g., "principal asks secretary to assign student to class," was entered. The last column was reserved for the researcher's comments about the interaction. This column included additional information, nonverbal signals, hunches, and so on. Another type of integration followed later through the construction of narratives of the whole observation incorporating taped data with notes. An index to the taped data was incorporated into the notes so that the original audio could be retrieved if necessary. Researcher's comments, hunches, or questions were also incorporated into the narrative enclosed in double parentheses.

Both of these renditions were coded and analyzed. Portions of them were transferred onto index cards under the different categories. A set of index cards was developed for each site. Hence it was possible to look at one site across categories or at one category across sites.

In addition to the observations at the schools sites, the researcher was invited to join the secretaries and their colleagues in District 1 during their informal monthly lunches. It was possible to attend three of these lunches during the observation period. In District 2 the researcher was invited to attend one of several meetings held annually between the district's central office staff and the school secretaries. The researcher also attended assorted school activities such as open house and fairs, and also occasionally accompanied individual secretaries on errands.

Documents related to the schools were also collected, principally staff bulletins and state reports. These documents represented the secretary's work and also gave indications of her role in the school. Recurring interactions and patterns were sought in the data. Each observation and notes from them gave rise to some ideas and hunches that led to further observations and eventually to the development of the codes used to organize the data. Codes were added when they were warranted by additional data. As observations increased, the recurrence of patterns indicated that the coding categories devised were appropriate. This was true with the exception of two new situations encountered in District 2. In one of these schools the secretary and principal met regularly and planned the week's work together. This was the only school where this situation occurred and required an independent subcategory. District 2 also held scheduled meetings between secretaries and district personnel. The one meeting attended by the researcher also required an independent subcategory.

Interviews

Interviews were conducted with each of the secretaries and principals at the six sites. The interviews were intended to provide data on the expressed perceptions of principals and secretaries about the secretary's job, the school and each other's roles. Interview instruments that followed parallel lines of questioning were used and allowed for within and across school comparisons.

Each of the secretaries and principals at the six targeted schools was individually interviewed. Two different, but parallel instruments were used.[2] With only a few exceptions, the questions asked of the principals were very similar to the ones asked of the secretaries. For example, secretaries were asked about their expectations for the school secretary's job before they assumed the position. Principals were asked a similar question about the principal's position. The interviews were semi-structured. The instruments ensured that all areas of interest would be covered, but spontaneity was encouraged during the session.

All but one of the interviews was conducted away from the school office in an effort to gain some distance from daily responsibilities as well as to avoid interruptions. Secretaries were interviewed in restaurants where a relaxed dinner followed. All but one of the principals were interviewed over breakfast or lunch; one chose to hold the interview at his office.

Analysis

The interview data were analyzed in two different ways. The use of parallel instruments made possible side-by-side comparisons of the expressed perceptions of principals and secretaries. It was also possible to analyze the expressed perceptions of this particular group of secretaries as well as of the group of principals.

Recurrent themes expressed by these individuals were sought through these analyses. Particular attention was paid to the metaphors used to describe the school secretary's role and/or the school environment itself. The side-by-side comparisons of principals and secretaries were especially useful in providing insight into the degree of compatibility existing between principal and secretary at each site. Did they use similar language in their descriptions of the school environment? Were their expectations for their complementary roles compatible? Did they provide similar examples and stories? Comparisons across sites provided evidence of possible similarities in the perceptions expressed by the principals as a group and those expressed by school secretaries.

QUANTITATIVE DATA

Survey

With the cooperation of the National Association of Educational Office Personnel (NAEOP), a national sample of elementary school secretaries was surveyed. The immediate past president and the incoming president both offered their cooperation, contributed their ideas, and reviewed successive drafts of the survey instrument. The association also provided a total of 724 mailing labels for all members of their Elementary School Secretaries Division. Surveys accompanied by a cover letter and one page of directions were mailed to all active members of the division.

The purpose of the survey was to gather demographic, attitudinal and working conditions data on elementary school secretaries all over the country. Seven-hundred and twenty-four surveys were sent out, and 350 questionnaires were returned (48%). Of these, 291 were suitable for analysis. Thirty-one surveys were either returned blank by people who at the time of the survey were in different positions, or were completed by people who were not elementary school secretaries. Some surveys were received after the coding and data analysis had been completed and could not be included. In addition to the 291 useful surveys returned, the six secretaries who were observed and interviewed were also asked to complete the survey. This brought the total number of surveys coded and analyzed to 297. Two open-ended questions in the survey received so many and such varied responses that they had to be analyzed separately through qualitative methods, that is, themes and patterns were identified and reported.

Designing the Instrument

The development of the survey involved four different drafts up to the pilot form. Additional revisions were made after the pilot form was completed, resulting in the final draft.

The first step in this process was a 2-hour interview with two experienced elementary school secretaries. They were asked to discuss their jobs and what they thought was important to know about them. They were also asked about typical problems they faced and about their own feelings about the job. There was no attempt to structure the interview; it was a free-flowing exchange of ideas. Afterward, the audiotapes of these interviews were analyzed and the comments of these two secretaries provided the structure for the first draft.

Another set of interviews was conducted with the immediate past and incoming presidents of the NAEOP. They were asked to suggest areas or questions that should be covered in the survey. They too contributed their ideas. These were added to the first draft; other revisions were made, and a second draft was prepared.

The second draft was circulated through the advisory committee of the NAEOP. They suggested revisions, added and/or deleted items, and contributed general comments. Their contributions led to another set of revisions and a third draft was produced. This one was sent to the two secretaries who had been interviewed originally, and to the NAEOP officers for their comments. Another revision took place after these consultations. At that point the survey was deemed ready for a pilot test.

Pilot Test

The pilot test was conducted through the courtesy and cooperation of the Arizona Educational Office Personnel Association (AEOP) during its 1984 Fall Conference. The group of elementary school secretaries attending the conference volunteered to participate in the pilot study after the purpose of the exercise was explained to them.

The pilot test was administered to the self-identified group of elementary school secretaries on November 3, 1984. This group of 26 actually included 4 school clerks and 1 aide as well as 21 elementary school secretaries. The results reported were mostly limited to the responses of the elementary school secretaries since they were the target group of interest for this study. The responses of the aide and clerks were analyzed separately and compared to those of the secretaries. These were clearly identified throughout. In most cases, differences between these groups were found to be slight.

The main purpose of the pilot test was to identify weak or poorly phrased questions, confusing items or format, and any other features of the draft survey that might interfere with the researcher's ability to collect useful information from the national survey. Participants were asked to add their own comments, and several did so.

As a result of this effort, several questions were found to be particularly troublesome. One question was not analyzed because the responses were so confused they were not likely to yield any useful information. These questions were modified in the final version. Perhaps because the time allowed for responding was insufficient, some respondents were not consistent throughout. Some questions were not answered completely and in some cases the number of respondents was very low.

The use of a small sample and of an instrument in draft form impeded drawing firm and fast conclusions from the results of the pilot test. A set of tentative conclusions was prepared and released with many cautions to the participants through the NAEOP leadership in the hopes that they might find them useful.

Survey Administration

The final form of the survey[3] was mailed out to the 724 elementary school secretaries who were members of the NAEOP in February 1985. Respondents were asked to return the completed questionnaires within 2 weeks. The vast majority of the completed questionnaires were returned during this time period. Since the return rate approached 50%, no follow-up was conducted.

The most surprising aspect of the responses was the enthusiasm the request seemed to elicit among participants. Their enthusiasm was evident in the marginal comments they added, the letters they enclosed, and particularly in their responses to the last two open-ended questions of the survey. Several NAEOP members who received the survey but did not fill out the questionnaire sent letters of apology explaining they were either in different positions or they were retired. Nonetheless, they submitted their own comments about their experiences as elementary school secretaries and/or about the survey itself.

The comments received were overwhelmingly positive about the survey, its contents, and thoroughness. Respondents were also enthusiastic about the study itself. Quite frequently they thanked the researcher for including them and extended their good wishes for a successful conclusion. Many offered to respond to additional queries. Another group asked for copies of the completed report. Although they had been promised anonymity, many included their names and addresses in their responses.

The responses to the open-ended questions were so voluminous as to make coding for quantitative analysis impractical. Those responses were removed from the quantitative analysis and analyzed instead as qualitative data. Marginal comments were also plentiful and helped to illuminate the coded responses. Although the literature does not mention the prevalence of marginal comments, informal conversations with other researchers suggest that the number and expansiveness of the comments contributed by these participants was unusual. These comments have been incorporated into the analysis of the quantitative data and contributed to its interpretation.

The question that was most troublesome for the participants in the pilot test was item 2 under Section IX, "Responsibilities." This item asked the secretaries to apportion percentages of time spent through the year to various tasks. The intent of the question was to identify and compare cyclical patterns in the activities of elementary school secretaries. The difficulties with the pilot version led to the inclusion of an explanatory paragraph preceding this item in the final form. This revision did not improve the responses, however. This item was deemed the most difficult by the respondents. Many did not complete it. Among those who did, several had arithmetical errors, and many others seemed to follow a pattern that might or might not correspond to reality. Almost all the negative comments made by the respondents were related to this question. They pointed out the difficulty of assigning proportions of time to tasks since they often overlapped. They also indicated that some of the tasks required a short, intensive period, while others were daily routines. In addition to these valid criticisms, the many missing and doubtful responses suggested that the question was inappropriate and should not have been included in the survey—at least not in that form. As a result, this item was eliminated from the analysis.

Format of the instrument

The survey was divided into 10 different sections, as follows:

1. Demographics—including age, sex, martial status, number of children, and so forth
2. Position—including questions about salary and title
3. Education and training
4. Experience
5. Inservice education—including services provided by the district as well as those provided by outside agencies
6. Office facilities—office size, equipment, and budget
7. School characteristics—state, urban, rural, socioeconomic status, ethnic balance, and so forth
8. Principal—including number of administrators, and a scale to rate the principal

9. Responsibilities—the tasks performed by the secretary, their preferences, their perceptions
10. Professional activities—membership and participation in the NAEOP

Unequal numbers of items were included within each section. The longest section, "Responsibilities," contained 10 items and the shortest section, "Inservice," contained only six items. The complete instrument was 18 pages long and took 45 to 60 minutes to complete. Some secretaries complained that the infamous Question IX, 2 took too long and added time to that figure. Most of the questions were forced choice; however, Likert scales and rank orderings were also used.

Three open-ended items were included. One asked respondents their reasons for joining the NAEOP. Those responses were categorized and entered in the data in quantified form. The other two open-ended items asked the secretaries: a) what they were most proud of in their work, and b) to add any additional comments they might have about their jobs or about the survey. The responses to these questions were overwhelming. Many respondents exceeded the space available and continued on the reverse side of the paper or added pages. The amount and variety of the responses made it necessary to consider and analyze these responses as qualitative data.

Analysis

The analysis of the data was straightforward, simple, and based on descriptive statistics. Frequency counts were used most often and were sufficient for many of the questions such as those answered by "yes" or "no." Means and standard deviations were also sought for a number of questions including age, salary, amount of money handled, and others.

Limitations

Almost all the respondents to this survey were members of the NAEOP division of elementary school secretaries at the time of the study. Nonmembers were represented by the six secretaries observed in their schools who also agreed to complete the survey and three other secretaries who received the survey from an enthusiastic respondent who copied it for them. All others were included in the membership lists of the NAEOP. It is not possible to know, since there is no comparable data, whether elementary school secretaries who are members of the NAEOP differ substantially from the universe of elementary school secretaries. Comparisons between the six observed secretaries and the total sample suggest few differences, but the inequality of sample size between the two groups limits this conclusion.

Assumptions

The cover letter to the survey asked that the person responding to the survey be the one having the "main responsibility in the elementary school office." Thus the researcher assumes that those responding to the survey were in fact working elementary school secretaries. Several completed surveys were eliminated because it was clear from the responses or the comments that the respondent did not hold such a position. Respondent's titles varied from Clerk 1 to Administrative Assistant and included Stenographer, Typist, and others. Where the title was ambiguous, the responses were analyzed for wide discrepancies that might indicate a different position. In most cases, the Additional Comments section at the end of the questionnaire provided clarification. Where doubt persisted, the responses were not included.

ARCHIVAL DATA

The purpose of the archival analysis was to find out what official documents (job descriptions) and textbooks for prospective administrators have to say about elementary school secretaries. Analyses of these sources permitted a comparison between official statements about elementary school secretaries and the reality as expressed by the secretaries and their principals and as perceived by the researcher. Two types of archival materials were analyzed for the study: job descriptions and textbooks of educational administration.

The job descriptions were submitted by 27 of the secretaries who responded to the survey. The cover letter accompanying the survey had requested respondents to submit their districts' job descriptions for the elementary school secretary's position if it was available.

The textbooks of educational administration were selected according to the recommendations of professors of educational administration. Ten textbooks were analyzed in the original report of this work (Casanova, 1985). The selection was updated for the purposes of this publication and resulted in nine textbooks, only two of which had been included in the first report.

Job Descriptions

These descriptions generally contain a formal statement of a district's expectations for elementary school secretaries. Since job descriptions are official documents that set the parameters considered appropriate for the elementary school secretary, they might be expected also to influence principal and secretary expectations and behavior in the school office.

The 27 job descriptions received represented 12 different states. The documents varied greatly in complexity. One was no more than a list of tasks with no elaboration. It contrasted with the most detailed form among those submitted, which was three pages long and included separate sections for "Scope of Responsibility," "Typical Duties" and "Preferred." Another one of the documents received could best be described as a job analysis statement.

Five categories were identified and constituted the framework for the analysis. These five categories were (a) title, (b) summary statement, (c) qualifications, (d) responsibilities, and (e) supervision. Patterns and themes were then identified within each of those categories and led to further subcategories.

Textbooks of Educational Administration

The following nine textbooks, listed in alphabetical order by author, were included in the analysis:

Campbell, R. F., Corbally, J. E., & Nystrand, R. O. (1983). *Introduction to education administration*. Boston: Allyn & Bacon.
Drake, T. L., & Roe, W. H. (1986). *The principalship. (3rd ed.)*. New York: Macmillan.
Hoy, W. K., & Miskel, C. G. (1987). *Educational administration: Theory, research and practice (3rd ed.)*. New York: Random House.
Kaiser, J. S. (1985). *The principalship*. Minneapolis, MN: Burgess.
Kimbrough, R. B., & Burkett, C. W. (1990). *The principalship: Concepts and practice*. Englewood Cliffs, NJ: Prentice-Hall.
Knezevich, S. J. (1984). *Administration of public education*. New York: Harper & Row.
Lipham, J. M., Rankin, R. E., & Hoe, Jr., J. A. (1985). *The principalship: Concepts, competencies and cases*. New York: Longman.
Saxe, R. W. (1980). *Educational administration today: An introduction*. Berkeley, CA: McCutcheon.
Ubben, G. C., & Hughes, L. W. (1989). *The principalship: Creative leadership for effective schools*. Boston: Allyn & Bacon.

Each of the textbooks was examined for any mention of the school office, or the school secretary. Sections on community relations and communication, included in most of these books, were also reviewed for any mention of the secretary's participation in these organizational activities. When references to the secretary were located within a text, those sections were analyzed for length, emphasis, and comprehensiveness of the description.

DATA INTEGRATION

The combination of methods used in this study provided a multidimensional view of the elementary school secretary. Findings from the different methods were triangulated to ascertain the consistency of the data. Comparisons of the findings from the four different data sources also led to the identification of similarities that might justify generalizations from the samples to the universe of elementary school secretaries. Given that each of these sets of data was gathered at a different distance from the source (observations, interviews, survey, content analysis), it was also possible to ascertain the degree of compatibility between the more distant and general levels and the more particular and specific ones. The combination of data sets also enabled the researcher to ascertain whether the views expressed through self-report measures were consistent with the observations made at the school sites. The study also made it possible to determine whether reports from the field were echoed in the literature used to prepare school administrators and in official job descriptions. The findings from these different data sets are brought together and integrated in the concluding chapter.

NOTES

1. The mobility ratio, that is, the rate of turnover of each school, was computed by dividing the sum of the total number of entrants and the total number of transfers out during the 1984 school year by the 1985 October enrollment (1984 entrants + 1984 losses, divided by October 1985 enrollment).

2. Copies of the interview instruments may be obtained directly from the author: Dr. Ursula Casanova, Division of Educational Leadership, Arizona State University, Tempe, AZ 85287-2411.

3. Copies of the survey instrument may be obtained directly from the author at the above address.

References

Adkinson, J. A. (1981, Fall). Women in School Administration: A review of the research. *Review of Educational Research, 5*(1), 311-343.

Anderson, M. E. (1988). Inducting principals: How school districts help beginners succeed. *Oregon School Study Council Bulletin, 32, 2.*

Baird, M. E. (1929, September). School secretary—her job. *American School Board Journal, 79*, 45-47.

Barr, R., Dreeben, R., & Wiratachi, N. (1983). *How schools work.* Chicago: The University of Chicago Press.

Bierly, M. (1946, December). The school secretary. *Nation's Schools, 35*, 46.

Blumberg, A., & Greenfield, W. (1980). *The effective principal: Perspectives on school leadership.* Boston, MA: Allyn & Bacon.

Bureau of the Census (1985). *Statistical Abstracts of the U.S.* (105th ed.). Washington, DC: Government Printing Office.

Bureau of the Census (1975). *Historical Statistics of the United States—Part 1—Colonial times to 1970.* Washington, DC: Government Printing Office.

Bureau of Labor Statistics (1980, October). *Bulletin #2080.* Washington, DC: U.S. Department of Labor.

Campbell, R. F., Corbally, J. E., & Nystrand, R. O. (1983). *Introduction to educational administration.* Boston, MA: Allyn & Bacon.

Casanova, U. (1985). *Are you the office? A descriptive study of elementary school secretaries.* Unpublished doctoral dissertation, Arizona State University, Tempe.

Church, G. L. (1971). *A proposed junior college curriculum for the preparation and training of educational secretaries in Arkansas.* Unpublished doctoral dissertation, University of Arkansas.

Crompton, R., & Jones, G. (1984). *White collar proletariat: Deskilling and gender in clerical work.* London: Macmillan.

Cubberley, E. P. (1923). *Principal and his school.* NY: Houghton Mifflin.

Deal, T. E. (1985). The symbolism of effective schools. *The Elementary School Journal, 85*(5), 601-620.

Deaux, K., & Major, B. (1987). Putting gender into context: An interactive model of gender-related behavior. *Psychological Review, 94*(3), 369-389.

Doud, J. L. (1988). *The K-8 principal in 1988.* Alexandria, VA: National Association of Elementary School Principals.

Drake, T. L., & Roe, W. H. (1986). *The principalship,* (3rd ed.). New York: Macmillan.

Evans, M. K. (1987, Spring). Department secretaries: Unsung heroines in the resolution of professional-organization conflict. *Human Organization, 46*(1), 62-69.

Fuller, F. M., & Batchelder, M. B. (1953, January-February). Opportunities for women at the administrative level. *Harvard Business Review, 13*, 113-114.

Gilligan, C. (1982). *In a different voice.* Cambridge: Harvard University Press.

Gist, A. S. (1924, July). *Bulletin of the Department of Elementary School Principals: The Third Yearbook, 3*(4), 205-210.

Givens, W. E. (1926, July). A message of encouragement. *The National Secretary, 1*(1), 5.

Glenn, C. B. (1937, October). Greetings. *The National secretary, 3*(1), 3.

Goldhaber, G. M., Dennis, H. S., Ricketts, G. M., & Wiio, O. (1979). *Information strategies: New pathways to corporate power.* Englewood Cliffs, NJ: Prentice-Hall.

Goodykoontz, B., & Lane, J. A. (1938). *The elementary school principalship: Some aspects of its development and status.* Washington, DC: U.S. Department of the Interior.

Gorton, R. A., & McIntyre, K. E. (1978). *The senior high principalship: The effective principal.* Reston, VA: National Association of Secondary School Principals.

Graubard, S. R. (1981, Summer). America's public schools: Public and private. *Daedalus, 110*(3), v-xxiv.

Hager, J. L., & Scarr, L. E. (1983, February). Effective schools—effective principals: How to develop both. *Educational Leadership, 40*(5), 38-40.

Hannay, L. M., & Stevens, K. W. (1984). A guide through the jungle: The indirect curriculum influence of the principal. Paper presented at the annual meeting of the American Educational Research Association, New Orleans.

Hanson, M. (1984, Winter). Exploration of mixed metaphors in educational administration research. *Issues in Education, 2*(3), 167-185.

Hart, J. (1985). The secondary school secretary—some hidden and some developmental aspects of the secretary's role. *Educational Management and Administration, 13*, 131-139.

Hawley, W. D., Rosenholtz, S. J., Goodstein, H., & Elasselbring, T. (1984, Summer). Leadership and student learning. *Peabody Journal of Education, 61*(4), 53-83.

Henderson, L. (1929). Clerical service in city school systems. *Bulletin of the Department of Elementary School Principals, Eighth Yearbook* (pp. 318-326). Washington, DC: National Education Association.

Henderson, L. (1936). President's message. *The National Secretary, 1*(1), 3.

Henderson, L. (1937, October). President's message. *The National Secretary, 3*(1), 4-5.

Hoy, W. K., & Miskel, C. G. (1987). *Educational administration: Theory, research and practice* (3rd ed.). New York: Random House.

Iannaccone, L. (1978). School governance and its community sociopolitical structure. In R. G. Corwin & R. A. Edelfelt (Eds.), *Perspectives on organizations: Schools in the larger social order.* Washington, DC: American Association of Colleges for Teacher Education and the Association of Teacher Educators.

Ibsen, H. (1930). A Doll's House. In *The Memorial Edition of the Plays of Henrik Ibsen* (pp. 175-252). Oslo: Norwegian State Publications.

Jackson, T. E. (1976). *The leadership behavior and role expectations of elementary school principals as perceived by elementary school secretaries, building representatives, and principals.* Unpublished doctoral dissertation, University of Michigan, Ann Arbor.

Jacobson, P. B., Logsdon, J. D., & Wiegman, R. R. (1973). *The principalship: New perspectives* (3rd ed.). Englewood Cliffs, NJ: Prentice-Hall.

Jacobson, P. B., Reavis, W. C., & Logsdon, J. D. (1954). *The effective school principal.* Englewood Cliffs, NJ: Prentice-Hall.

Kaiser, J. S. (1985). *The principalship*. Minneapolis, MN: Burgess.

Kanter, R. M. (1977). *Men and women of the corporation*. New York: Basic Books.

Kimbrough, R. B., & Burkett, C. W. (1990). *The principalship: Concepts and practice*. Englewood Cliffs, NJ: Prentice-Hall.

Knezevich, S. J. (1984). *Administration of public education*. New York: Harper & Row.

Landis, E. H. (1938, April). A message of encouragement. *The National Secretary, 3*(1), 1.

Leithwood, K. A., & Montgomery, D. J. (1982, Fall). The role of the elementary school principal in program improvement. *Review of Educational Research, 52*(3), 309-339.

Lipham, J. M., Rankin, R. E., & Hoe, J. A. Jr. (1985). *The principalship: Concepts, competencies and cases*. New York: Longman.

Lobsenz, N. M., & Blackburn, C. W. (1968). *How to stay married*. New York: Cowles Books.

Lofland, L. H. (1975). The "thereness" of women: A selected review of urban sociology. In M. Millman & R. M. Kanter (Eds.), *Feminist perspectives on social life and social science*. New York: Anchor Press/Doubleday.

Lopata, H. Z., Miller, C. A., & Barnewolt, D. (1984). *City women: Work, jobs, occupations, careers*. New York: Praeger.

Lortie, D. C. (1977). Two anomalies and three perspectives. In R. G. Corwin & R. A. Edelfelt (Eds.), *Perspectives on organizations* (pp 20-38). Washington, DC: American Association of Colleges for Teacher Education and the Association of Teacher Educators.

March, J. G. (1974). analytical skills and the university training of educational administrators. *Journal of Educational Administration, 12*, 17-44.

March, J. G. (1978, February). American public school administration: A short analysis, *School Review*, 217-250.

March, J. G., & Olsen, J. P. (1979). *Ambiguity and choice in organizations*. Bergen, Norway: Universitets Forlaget.

Martin, T. D. (1937, October). School secretaries and the National Education Association. *The National Secretary, 3*(1), 5-6.

McClure, W. (1921, October). The work outlined. *Bulletin of the Department of Elementary School Principals, 3*(1), 3-40.

McClure, W. (1930, April). The duties of elementary school clerks in Seattle. *Bulletin of the Department of Elementary School Principals, 8*, 250-257.

McClure, W. (1930, July). The duties of elementary school clerks in Seattle. *Elementary School Principals, The Ninth Yearbook*, 10.

McGill, E. P. (1926, July). A study of clerical help for elementary school principals. *Bulletin of the Department of Elementary School Principals: The Fifth Yearbook, 5*(4), 229-234.

Mills, C. W. (1953). *White collar: The American middle classes*. Cambridge: Oxford University Press.

Morris, V. C., Crowson, R. L., Hurwitz, E., & Porter-Gehrie, C. (1981). *The urban principal: Discretionary decision-making in a large educational organization*. Chicago: University of Illinois at Chicago Circle.

Morse, N. C. (1953). *Satisfaction in the white collar job*. Ann Arbor, MI: University of Michigan.

National Center for Education Statistics. (1985). *Digest of Educational Statistics, 1983-84*. Washington, DC: Government Printing Office.

National Education Association Departmental Status for the National Association of School Secretaries. (1944, October). *The National Secretary, 10*(1), 14.

National Education Association Research Division. (1927, January-December). Median salary paid city elementary school teachers in 1926-1927. *Journal of the National Education Association, 16*(3), 83.

National Education Association. (1928, April). *Bulletin of the Department of Elementary School Principals: The Seventh Yearbook.* Washington, DC: Author.

National Education Association. (1947). Department Reports. *Addresses and proceedings of the eighty-fifth annual meeting held at Cincinnati, OH, July 7-11.* Washington, DC: Author.

Ortiz, F. I., & Marshall, C. (1988). Women in educational administration. In N. J. Boyan (Ed.), *Handbook of Research on Educational Administration* (pp. 123-142). NY: Longman.

Pharis, W. L., & Zakariya, S. B. (1979). *The elementary school principalship in 1978: A research study.* Arlington, VA: National Association of Elementary School Principals.

Priest, J. (1972, August). Mr. Administrator, let me help you. *The School Administrator, 7.*

Rahe, H. (1960). The school secretary. *American Business Education, 16*(3), 156-161.

Report of the Committee on Standards and Training for the Elementary School Principals of the National Education Association. (1928, April). *Bulletin of the Department of Elementary School Principals: The Seventh Yearbook, 7*(3), 166-167.

Rimer, A. (1984, Fall). Elementary school secretary: Informal decision maker. *Educational Horizons, 63*(1), 16-18.

Russell, R. V. (1973). *The role of the school secretary as perceived by principals, teachers, and other school secretaries.* Unpublished doctoral dissertation, Northern Arizona University.

Rutter, M., Maughan, B., Mortimore, P., & Ouston, J. (1979). *Fifteen thousand hours: Secondary schools and their effects on children.* Cambridge: Harvard University Press.

Sargent, I. G. (1923, October). Report of the Committee on Educational Progress: Salaried clerical and supervisory assistance. *Bulletin of the Department of Elementary School Principals, 3*(1), 35-39.

Saxe, R. W. (1980). *Educational administration today: An introduction.* Berkeley, CA: McCutcheon.

Schmuck, R. A., Runkel, P. J., Arends, J. H., & Arends, I. A. (1977). *The second handbook of organizational development in schools.* Palo Alto, CA: Mayfield.

Sergiovanni, T. J. (1984). Leadership as cultural expression. In T. J. Sergiovanni & J. I. Corbally (Eds.), *Leadership and organizational culture: New perspectives on administrative theory and practice* (pp. 105-114). Urbana, IL: University of Illinois Press.

Sexson, J. A. (1938, October). A message of encouragement. *The National Secretary.* San Antonio, TX: National Association of School Secretaries.

Shuttle, N. A., Kendrick, D. T., & Sadalla, E. K. (1985). The search for predictable settings: Situational prototypes, constraint, and behavioral variation. *Journal of Personality and Social Psychology, 49,* 121-128.

Simon, T. I. (1972). *A study of the motivation of school secretaries.* Unpublished doctoral dissertation, University of Southern California.

Stowell, R. T. (1974). *Behavior of selected elementary school secretaries: A study of decision patterns in the absence of the principal.* Unpublished doctoral dissertation, Temple University.

Sweeney, C. (1987, January). What does your school secretary really want? *Thrust, 16*(4), 49-51.

Tepperman, J. (1976). *Not servants, not machines: Office workers speak out.* Boston: Beacon.

The National Secretary (1937, January). Biography of Louise Henderson (p. 3), and biography of Margaret Kernan (p. 7). Author.

Ubben, G. C., & Hughes, L. W. (1989). *The principalship: Creative leadership for effective schools.* Boston, MA: Allyn & Bacon.

U.S. Department of Labor (1975). *Handbook on women workers* (pp. 91-92). Washington, DC: Government Printing Office.

Vinnicombe, S. (1980). *Secretaries, management, and organizations.* London: Heinemann Editorial Books.

Williamson, T. R., & Karras, E. J. (1970). Job satisfaction variables among female clerical workers. *Journal of Applied Psychology, 54*(4), 343-346.

Wolcott, H. F. (1973). *The man in the principal's office.* New York: Holt, Rinehart & Winston.

Index

DATE DUE